SMASHING TIMES

A HISTORY OF THE IRISH WOMEN'S SUFFRAGE MOVEMENT
1889 - 1922

Rosemary Cullen Owens

First published in 1984 by
ATTIC PRESS
48 Fleet Street,
Dublin 2.

British Library Cataloguing in Publication Data
Owens, Rosemary Cullen
    Smashing Times: a history of the Irish Women
    Suffrage Movement 1889-1922

    1. Women – Suffrage – Ireland – History
    i. Title
    324.6'23'09417   JN1525

    ISBN 0-946211-07-8
    ISBN 0-946211-08-6 pbk

Cover design: Keggy Carew
Typesetting: Design and Art Facilities in 10pt Palatino
Printing: Irish Printers
This book has been produced in its entirity in Ireland.

The Publisher gratefully acknowledges the assistance of the
copyright owners of illustration material reproduced in this book, in
particular the National Library of Ireland, Andree Sheehy
Skeffington, Library of the Society of Friends, I.T.G.W.U., Dublin
Corporation, Irish Times and The Royal Society of Antiquaries of
Ireland.

To my Parents

It is time to effect a revolution in female manners – time to restore to (women) their lost dignity – and make them, as a part of the human species, labour by reforming themselves to reform the world.

Mary Wollstonecraft *A Vindication of the Rights of Woman* (1792).

ACKNOWLEDGEMENTS

I would like to thank the following publishers for permission to quote from books published by them: Bantam Books Inc. for *The Feminist Papers* (ed.) by Alice S. Rossi; University of Massachusetts Press for *Constance de Markievicz in the Cause of Ireland* by Jacqueline Van Voris; Croom Helm Ltd. for *The Feminists: Women's Emancipation Movements in Europe, American and Australasia 1840-1920* by Richard J. Evans; Routledge & Kegan Paul Ltd. for *Rise Up Women! The Militant Campaign of the Women's Social and Political Union 1903-1914* by Andrew Rosen; Hutchinson & Co. Ltd. for *Unshackled* by Christabel Pankhurst; Appletree Press Ltd. for *The Rise of the Irish Working Class* by Dermot Keogh; Gill & McMillan for *The Founding of Dáil Éireann: Parliament and Nation-Building* by Brian Farrell; Doubleday & Co. Inc. for *Life and the Dream* by Mary Colum; Ganesh & Co. for *We Two Together* by J.H. & M.E. Cousins; Kilkenny People Ltd. for *Cumann na mBan and the Women of Ireland* by Lil Conlon; Arlen House for articles by J.J. Lee, Mary E. Daly & Maurice Manning in *Women in Irish Society, The Historical Dimension.*

I would also like to thank the following institutions for permission to quote from collections in their possession: The National Library of Ireland for the Sheehy Skeffington papers and Women's Suffrage Exhibition material; University of Dublin, Trinity College for the John Dillon papers; The State Paper Office of Ireland for General Prisons Board, Suffragette Papers 1912-14 & Chief Secretary's Office, Police & Crime Reports 1886-1915; Library of the Society of Friends, Eustace St., Dublin for Haslam documentation; British Museum for Henry Devenish Harben correspondence 1912-14.

The following individuals deserve special thanks: Andree Sheehy Skeffington for access to the Sheehy Skeffington papers and for her consistent co-operation during the course of my research; Eibhlin Breathnach for permission to quote from her M.A. thesis 'A History of the Movement for Women's Higher Education in Dublin 1860-1912; the women currently participating in the Women in Community Publishing course being run by Irish Feminist Information for their help in collating photographic and other illustratory material; Mary Paul Keane and Roisin Conroy for their courage in deciding to publish this book and their help and patience during the course of its writing; Orla Taaffe for helping me cope with the various crises which occurred; finally my family for their tremendous encouragement and support, with a special thanks to Tom, Simon and David Owens.

Rosemary Cullen Owens November 1984

CONTENTS

ABBREVIATIONS

I.C.W.S.A.	Irish Catholic Women's Suffrage Association.
I.W.S.L.G.A.	Irish Women's Suffrage and Local Government Association.
I.W.F.L.	Irish Women's Franchise League.
I.W.S.F.	Irish Women's Suffrage Federation.
I.W.R.L.	Irish Women's Reform League.
I.W.S.S.	Irish Women's Suffrage Society.
C.&U.W.S.A.	Conservative and Unionist Women's Suffrage Association.
C.L.W.S.	Church League for Women's Suffrage.
W.S.P.U.	Women's Social and Political Union.
N.U.W.S.S.	National Union of Women's Suffrage Societies.

ILLUSTRATIONS

Introduction

The demand for equality between the sexes and for female participation in all areas of life is not a new phenomenon. The first such demand was voiced in Dublin over one hundred years ago. In Ireland, as in England, educational opportunities for women improved in the last quarter of the nineteenth century. Such opportunities only served to emphasise the limited sphere open to women. Not only were women prevented from holding public office, but they were not allowed a voice in choosing their parliamentary representative. Consequently they had no say in the making of laws to which they were held accountable.

The 1870s saw the first attempt at organising Irish women to demand equality. Great emphasis was placed on obtaining equal political rights for women. Pioneers of the women's movement believed that until women had full political equality with men, women's equality in other areas could not be guaranteed. Taking place, as it did, against a background of Victorian society and values, the early women's movement simultaneously reflected that society and challenged it. While the demand for women's political equality shocked many Victorians, that demand was couched in terms acceptable to the social values of the time. Therefore, the demand for the local and parliamentary vote for women was based on the property qualifications applicable. At a time when many men were without a vote, qualified women sought parity with their male counterparts – not adult suffrage. In the early years of the twentieth century this tacit acceptance of a class system was to be challenged by many liberal and socialist reformers who criticised suffrage campaigners as advocating votes for ladies, not for women. The influence of such reformers was to be seen in many of the new women's groups which developed during the first decade of the twentieth century. Some of these groups allied with the labour movement and sought wide-ranging reform of societal structures. All women's groups believed – naively perhaps to modern eyes – that the granting of votes to women would ensure female influence in legislation affecting all areas of women's life, and women's participation in public life.

By the early twentieth century a body of educated articulate women had emerged who were prepared to endorse their beliefs with militant action. At first this consisted of heckling politicians whenever possible on the issue of votes for women, and later developed into symbolic acts against government property as a protest against government intransignence on the issue. Between 1912-14 there were thirty-six convictions of Irish women for such activities, many of whom went on hunger-strike in support of their demands. Feelings ran so high during these years on the question of votes for women that in addition to the various women's suffrage societies which emerged, a men's league for women's suffrage was formed in England, as was an anti-women's suffrage society – composed of women and men – the latter with a branch in Ireland. A new word was introduced to describe this new breed of militant women – suffragette – a nickname created by the English press. This word applied solely to militant women, the older term – sufffragist – being used to describe any person, female or male, involved in the women's suffrage campaign.

The campaign for women's suffrage in Ireland had many factors and influences to contend with which differentiated it from the English movement. Differing social structures, religious and political affliations are reflected in the variety of societies which evolved in Ireland between 1908-14. Most of the Irish women whose names have become well known in other connections, were at one time active in the movement. A random sample reveals names such as Dr. Kathleen Lynn, Louie Bennett, Helen Chenevix, Constance Markievicz, Professor Mary Hayden, Hanna Sheehy Skeffington, 'Somerville & Ross', Katherine Tynan, Eva Gore-Booth, Mary Colum, Mary McSwiney, Winifred Carney, Jennie Wyse-Power. The majority of active suffragists however, were not well known people, but ordinary women – and some men – who recognised the injustice of relegating woman to a special sphere, thereby depriving her of the advantages and responsibilities of citizenship. To them the vote was the symbol of citizenship and an instrument of power. From 1912 political developments in Ireland placed great strain on the unity of the women's movement. Increasingly the energies of many suffragists were drawn into the political struggles of the time. Unfortunately, as will be seen in the following pages, such political involvement too often required the suppression – or at least postponement of feminist demands. That it took some fifty years for such demands to be voiced again by Irishwomen is perhaps a lesson to be noted by their successors.

Rosemary Cullen Owens November 1984

Seeds of Unrest

*The sex of a women, though it may be a
misfortune is not a crime.* Edward Gibson 1863 [1]

In the latter half of the nineteenth century there developed in
England and Ireland a series of movements aimed at improving
the social, economic and political status of women. Similar
movements were also developing throughout Europe and
America. Initially such movements started as campaigns for
improved educational and employment opportunities for
single middle-class women. To this was added the demand for
property rights for married women, female representation on
public boards and local authorities, the right to vote in local
elections, and ultimately the demand for the parliamentary
vote. The history of such movements has been described as 'the
history of a progressively widening set of objectives'. [2] The
pressure which developed for such changes had a mainly
middle class base. Indeed the emergence of the middle classes
is often cited as the most significant development underlying
the rise of feminism, and the activities pursued by women's
groups up until the early twentieth century generally reflected
their middle-class composition. Outside Ireland this was to
change in the early 1900s as working-class women from highly
industrialised areas became involved.

The passing of the Act of Union in 1800 established the
United Kingdom of Great Britain and Ireland. This involved the
loss of Ireland's native parliament and the absorption of the
Irish parliamentary representatives into the Westminster
parliament. From 1800 until Ireland achieved independence in
1921 all laws governing Ireland would emanate from that
parliament. During the nineteenth century a gradual extension
and democratisation of local and parliamentary franchises
occured in the United Kingdom. The three major extensions of
parliamentary franchise occured in 1832, 1868 and 1884.
Changes in the structure of English society were primarily
responsible for such extensions. The development of large
urban centres and industrialised areas resulting from changing
patterns of industry and employment meant a significant shift
from the land to towns and cities for an increasing proportion

of the population. Whereas up to 1832 parliamentary power had been vested in wealthy landowners and aristocrats, these reform acts gradually extended the parliamentary vote to other sections of the population. The principal groups to be included were the new prosperous middle-class merchants and industrialists, professional groups and, increasingly over the years, larger numbers of the urban and agricultural workforce. However, not until 1872 did secret balloting become law, enabling workers in towns and country to use their vote freely without fear of reprisals from employer or landlord. Despite such advances, however, the parliamentary franchise still retained two of its original disabilities at the end of the century. It was primarily property-based rather than person-based, which meant that significant levels of the population were still without a vote. In effect there developed household rather than adult suffrage, certain minimum property qualifications being necessary in order to vote. In addition all women, irrespective of whether or not they fulfilled the property qualifications, were excluded. The result was that in 1911, in the United Kingdom as a whole, only about thirty percent of the total adult population, and about sixty percent of the male adult population could vote at parliamentary elections. In Ireland the level was somewhat lower, the proportion of adult males enfranchised in the four Dublin city parliamentary divisions in 1911 varying from forty-one to fifty percent.[3]

The Reform Act of 1832 had, by its use of the words 'male person', specifically introduced sex discrimination into electoral qualifications, and this was extended in 1835 to include local and municipal government franchises. This act has been described as planting the seed of later female suffrage agitation.[4] Up to 1832 women in England and Ireland were prevented from voting by custom only, and in medieval times many qualified women had in fact exercised their right to vote. From 1832, however, women were prohibited from voting by law.

It is against a background of gradually extending eligibility for the parliamentary vote allied to the inherent changes brought about in the organisation of political parties that the ninteenth century campaign for women's suffrage should be viewed. This movement originated, as had original moves for extension of the male franchise, within the middle-classes. The life of middle and upper-class women in Ireland and England in Victorian times was restricted by custom and law. Such educational opportunities as existed were of a limited nature and higher education was not deemed necessary or even advisable for a woman. A woman of these classes was not expected to earn her own living, but to remain dependant upon a man, first as a daughter and later as wife. If a woman married, her estate passed to her husband as, prior to the passing of the Married Women's Property Acts of 1870, 1874 and 1882, married women could not own property. A women's rights over her children were also limited. By a law of 1839 a mother had a right to custody of her child only up to the age of seven years. Not until 1873 was this changed to allow a mother custody of her child up to sixteen years. However, a significant number of Victorian women did not marry, and as Andrew Rosen points out in his study of the English suffrage movement:

> In the 1850s and 1860s, there was simply no career offering any degree of intellectual scope, pecuniary reward, and social respectability open to an unmarried middle class woman, unless she happened to have special artistic talent. It was primarily as a reaction against the manifest lack of opportunities for unmarried middle class women that organised feminism began in Britain. [5]

Despite improvements in the status of women during the course of the century, notably in the field of education, and the eventual extension of the local government vote to some women, right into the twentieth century, women did not possess the parliamentary franchise. Consequently they had no direct voice in the making of laws to which they were held accountable, and which often directly discriminated against them. They were governed by laws made by men alone. Many women came to look upon attainment of the parliamentary vote, not merely as their right as citizens, but as the only effective way to influence law-making in their favour.

While the laws governing nineteenth-century Ireland and England were to a large extent similar, the social and political circumstances were quite different. Nineteenth-century Ireland was predominantly rural in character. In 1841 only twenty percent of the population lived in towns (by 1971 this had risen to fifty-nine percent).[6] There were only three towns with more than 50,000 inhabitants – Dublin, Belfast and Cork. The dependence of the overwhelming majority of Irish people on the land for subsistence explains the horrific consequences of the great famine of 1845-48. That famine is generally regarded as a major source of change in Irish society. By 1841 the population of country had steadily increased to over the eight million people. Over two-thirds of these were dependent on argiculture for their livelihood, and the potato formed the staple diet of the majority. Minor potato famines due to blight had occured before in Ireland, but were regional and of short duration. The blight which occurred in 1845-46, however, was to be general and devastating in its effect. By 1851 the population of the country had steadily increased to over eight some two million people having been lost through death and emigration.

The events of these years were to reverberate throughout Irish political, social and economic life. The most immediate and discernible effect was on the lifestyle of the rural population. A trend towards larger farms developed, necessitating a shift away from the pre-famine practice of sub-dividing family land into small holdings. This practice had facilitated early marriages, and no doubt contributed to the population increase. Simultaneously, the collapse of domestic 'cottage' industries through growing industrialisation removed the main source of independent income from many rural women. In Britain the decline of domestic textile industries through the spread of the factory system was compensated for by the emergence of factory employment. In Ireland this did not happen outside of north-east Ulster . As a result of these factors the marriage rate fell. By 1926 about twenty-five percent of Irishwomen remained unmarried at the age of forty-five, compared with about ten percent before the famine.[7] The spread of the dowry system was a further disincentive, as farmers were reluctant to dower more than one daughter. Increasing life expectancy meant that sons had to wait longer to inherit their farm and marry. Whereas before the famine about twenty percent of husbands were ten years older than their wives, by the early twentieth century this had risen to about fifty percent.[8] The number of women within the agricultural community fell much more sharply than did the number of men. By 1912 they accounted for about one-fifth of the total, compared to one-third in 1871.[9] Faced with poor marriage prospects and virtually no employment opportunities, increasingly large numbers of women left rural Ireland, some going to cities like Dublin where domestic service was the main employment, but the majority to England and America. The emigration of young Irish women worried some clergy. Joseph Lee in his essay 'Women and the Church since the Famine' quotes Fr Guinan who wrote in 1903:

> How blessed would have been the lot of an Irish girl, the poor betrayed victim of hellish agencies of vice, had she remained at home and passed her days in the poverty, aye and wretchedness, of a mud wall cabin – a wife and mother, mayhap – her path in life smoothened by the blessed influences of religion and domestic peace until it ended at a green old age.[10]

However, as Lee points out, it was precisely because the country girl had seen no chance of becoming a wife and mother that she had emigrated at all. Similarly, Fr Michael O'Riordan, rector of the Irish College in Rome, claimed that 'genuine Irish Catholic girls are never short of proposals to share a home with them'. Here again Lee points out that that is exactly what many genuine Irish catholic – and protestant – girls were short of, proposals, remarking caustically that 'genuine christianity provided little competition for a full purse on the marriage market'.

Margaret MacCurtain has pointed to the extraordinary post-famine wave of devotional piety which found its focus in Mary, Mother of Sorrows. In her study 'Towards an Appraisal of the Religious Image of Women' she notes that such a model was particularly appropriate for a generation of women who became widows at a relatively young age on the death of their elderly husbands. This model also reflected the endemic sadness in rural Irish women who knew that by the age of eighteen or nineteen most of their children would have emigrated. In pursuing this theory MacCurtain points to the image of sorrowful Irish womanhood found in the works of playwrights John Synge and Sean O'Casey and in the poems of Padraic Pearse.[11]

Employment opportunities for women in urban Ireland during the nineteenth century were also severely limited, but Mary E. Daly has highlighted some areas open to such women in her essay 'Women in the Irish Work-force from Pre-Industrial to Modern Times'. Some opened 'huckster' shops, engaged in street selling, helped fathers or husbands to run shops or public houses, worked as dressmakers, charwomen, washerwomen or kept lodgers, or did some industrial work from home. She points out, however, that although many women, married and unmarried, contributed substantially to family income, such involvement did not bring any increased status:

> Because prosperous middle and upper class women very consciously neither contributed to family income, nor to household chores, the role of women who worked, particularly those who earned an income, tended to be downgraded, and the woman of leisure who devoted herself to accomplishments, or failing that, a full-time home-maker, became the ideal for many. Such ideals gradually permeated Irish society.[12]

The resulting low status accorded to women's work had far-reaching implications. The majority of women worked out of necessity rather than choice, being casual rather than permanent workers. Their consequent vulnerability and rapid turnover made them difficult to organise. As a result, women's work was generally classified as unskilled or semi-skilled, even though, as Daly points out, many of the tasks they carried out in linen mills or with the sewing machines required considerable expertise. These conditions of low wages and exploitation incurred the wrath of male workers by driving down wages, which further convinced them that the proper place for women was in the home.

In addition to the legal, economic and social disabilities of women another major factor to be considered was the influence of the churches. In England, Europe and America the demand for female equality found a solid base in predominantly protestant communities. In Ireland the role of the catholic church in formulating and influencing popular ideas on the role and status of women was immense. It is significant that the women's movement was least successful in countries with a predominantly catholic and rural population. In post-famine Ireland the proportion of clergy to laity began to rise dramatically. In 1840 there was one catholic priest to about 3,500 lay people; in 1960 there was one to every 600.[13] The vast proportion of these were drawn from comfortable farming backgrounds. This development coincided with a general desexualisation of women in the Irish imagination. Eibhlin Breathnach, in her study of the movement for women's higher education in Dublin, states that:

> The notion of women in nineteenth century Ireland was
> rooted in the twin influences, one deriving from the
> catholic devotion to Our Lady, virgin and mother,
> encompassed in which was the polar opposite figure Eve,
> and the other was drawn from the Victorian ideal of
> service and devotion to men, personified by the sombre
> persona of Victoria herself.[14]

She notes that this drawing of the image of Eve highlighted the reverence to Our Lady, placing women on such an ideological pedestal that no middle ground for ordinary struggling women remained. She also makes the point that underpinning such an outlook was a view of sex which equated it, for all practical purposes, with sin: a woman's sexuality at best was for the purpose of procreation and at worst was the cause of man's downfall. Such notions found widespread acceptance in a predominantly rural society whose economic security was seen to depend on more infrequent and late marriages, sex posing greater threats to stability than the landlord. The permeation of such values to the urban milieu was ascribed to the twin agencies of church and school.[15]

The increasing involvement of the church in education, through the national schools, training colleges and the growing number of convent secondary schools, cemented such images of woman, justifying her secondary position as one fixed by God. Although the number of female teachers increased after the famine, they inevitably indoctrinated their pupils with the attitudes of their class and church. Lee states that literacy, for all its ultimate emancipatory potential, became in the short term another instrument for stifling independent thought, 'Dutiful woman teachers, including many dedicated nuns, taught girls obedience, docility and resignation to the role assigned to them by a male providence.'[16] He also notes that protestant clergy of the time were equally preoccupied with sex, suspecting both it and catholicism with equal fervour. As Eibhlin Breathnach concludes, the only salvation for woman in such a situation lay in realising the ideal by becoming either mother or virgin, wife or nun.

In fact, the nineteenth century saw the proliferation of female religious orders in Ireland, and increasingly girls' education came into the hands of nuns. Elements of class distinction developed as certain orders catered for certain social classes. The convent itself now became one of the few career options for women. Even then there were distinctions – most convents required a dowry for one to become a community sister; with no dowry one became a lay sister doing the menial work. It has been argued that the growth of such religious orders provided a rare opportunity for able women to show their talent for leadership, and that could certainly be said of the founders and of many of the sisters. But generally, as Lee points out, nuns were dehumanised in the public imagination to a far greater extent than priests.

The second half of the nineteenth century witnessed two abortive attempts at revolution against English rule in Ireland. Although both the Young Irelanders of 1848-49, and the Fenians (the Irish Republican Brotherhood) in 1867 were both unsuccessful in their attempted rebellions, they left a legacy of republican idealism which was to be picked up later in the century by a new generation of separatists. From 1870 constitutional politicians came to place their trust in the attainment of Home Rule for Ireland. The Home Rule movement, from 1877 led by Charles Stewart Parnell, a wealthy landowner from Avondale, County Wicklow, sought the establishment of an Irish parliament with control over all domestic affairs. In the years leading up to the outbreak of World War I in 1914 the issue of Home Rule for Ireland was to be inextricably linked with the by then vociferous demand by English suffragettes for parliamentary votes for women. That demand was also to be made by Irish women.

THE SUFFRAGETTE SCARE IN DUBLIN.

Discovery by the Intilligince Department of a Disguised Militant Selling Bombs

Cartoon from *The Lepracaun* 1912.

The Awakening

A woman's mission is to be true to her own womanhood, and surely no nobler portion of this mission is there than the exalting of men. [1]

In 1820 the English philosopher and reformer, James Mill, wrote that political rights could be removed without inconvenience from certain classes of people, including women, 'the interests of almost all of whom are involved in that of their fathers or in that of their husbands'. [2] This provoked the publication in London in 1825 of the first definitive work advocating female suffrage. William Thompson from Cork, socialist and pioneer of the co-operative movement, and Anna Wheeler, the daughter of an Irish protestant archbishop and a godchild of Henry Grattan, were the authors of this work, cumbersomely entitled *An appeal of one-half of the human race, women, against the pretensions of the other half, men, to retain them in political and hence in civil and domestic slavery*. In this it was stated that:

> All women and particularly women living with men in marriage... having been reduced by the want of political rights to a state of helplessness and slavery... are more in need of political rights than any other portion of human beings.

At this time no movement towards attaining such equality emerged. During the first half of the nineteenth century women's groups in Ireland, where they existed, concentrated on various charitable works usually aimed at improving the condition of the peasantry. [3] The members of such groups were generally of upper middle class and aristocratic background. The post-famine years saw a further development of such works, including the establishment of schools to teach crafts to Irish girls to enable then to earn their livelihood. [4] In time some of these schools were handed over to local convents who continued the tradition. One such instance concerned Anna Haslam, a quaker from Youghal, who was to be prominent in the women's suffrage campaign. She taught lacemaking and knitting to local young women and established a thriving lacemaking industry, which she later handed over to the Presentation nuns.[5]

Gradually, however, some of the women involved in such societies began to look for more challenging opportunities. In England the changing structure of society manifested by a strong and growing middle-class led to demands for increased job opportunities for the unmarried and widowed women of that class. One of the first obstacles encountered in this quest was the inadequate nature of women's education. Girls were taught accomplishments, not skills. Two developments occurred. A number of agencies were established to further the employment of middle class women, some of which provided classes and instruction in the skills necessary for such positions as were then available, mainly office and craft work, in addition to the traditional career of governess. Simultaneously there emerged a demand for better education for girls and their admission to higher education. An Irish branch of the Society for Promoting the Employment of Educated Women was established in Dublin in 1861. The society sought to overcome the lack of business training available for women, establishing classes in book-keeping, writing and arithmetic. Instruction in the use of the sewing machine was provided, as were classes in law-copying, lithography, etching and wood engraving. Women were also placed in hospitals for training as nurses. The London branch of the society operated an emigration agency which selected women for positions in the colonies, and the Dublin branch worked in co-operation with this.[6]

In 1866, when a new franchise reform bill, which would further extend the male franchise, was imminent, the first petition seeking female suffrage was presented to the House of Commons. It was presented by John Stuart Mill, son of James Mill, who, unlike his father was a lifelong champion of women's rights, and included the signatures of twenty-five Irishwomen, one of whom was Anna Haslam.[7] The following year the first debate on female suffrage in the House of Commons occurred with Mill's proposed amendment to the 1867 Representation of the People Act. This proposed to replace the word 'man' in the act by the word 'person'. The amendment failed. According to an act of 1850 the word 'man' was deemed to include females,

Anne Haslam.

unless the contrary was expressly provided. As a consequence over seven thousand women claimed to be placed on the register, but after legal proceedings their claim was refused by the courts.[8] In 1869 the municipal (local government) franchise was granted to English women and the first in a series of married women's property acts was passed in 1870.

A constant stream of petitions regarding women's suffrage was sent to MPs and the Houses of Parliament over the following years. In 1870 the first woman suffrage bill passed its second reading in the House of Commons but was prevented from progressing any further by the Liberal government. By April 1875 the majority voting against another woman suffrage bill was only thirteen, despite two very stiff whips. This created so much unease amongst opponents of female suffrage in the House of Commons that a committee was formed 'for maintaining the integrity of the franchise'.[9]

While the pressure for parliamentary change was developing in England, the question of woman and her place was not totally ignored in Irish circles. An unsigned article in the *Dublin University Magazine* of May 1839 criticised the independent character of French women, noting thankfully that:

> On the contrary, there is no free country where the
> women have less of a separate existence than in Ireland.
> The Irishwoman, taking rank for rank is incomparably
> more cultivated than the French, though with far less
> pretension to knowledge.

Twenty years later another unsigned article in the same
periodical on the question of female education declared:

> No education will ever fit them for the peculiar pursuits of
> men; but it will make them truer helpmates for men.... we
> do wish our women to be nobly educated, purely
> educated; to be taught to think well and think strongly;
> and then the more they know the more silent and humble
> will they become, for all real knowledge has that stillness
> of the ocean which is gained from depth. [10]

One can understand why John Stuart Mill, writing to Anna
Haslam's husband in 1867 on the feasibility of starting a
suffrage society in Dublin, concluded that 'the immediate
prospects are not encouraging'. [11]

However, ideas of change were taking hold in some quarters
and in 1870 a paper read to the Cork Literary and Scientific
Society on the emancipation of women noted that 'an
impending change is manifest in the present social and political
position of women'. Interest in the subject was apparently so
great that we are told that a debate which followed the paper
lasted four nights. The author, John Walter Bourke, stated that
'It is now become a national question on which definite opinion
must be formed.' [12] Indeed the groundwork for such changes
was being prepared. In 1870 an English women's suffrage
journal reported that numerous petitions from all over Ireland
had been received at the House of Commons seeking women's
franchise and the married women's property bill. Over the next
few years there are reports of suffrage meetings held in various
parts of the country, including Dublin, Cork, Belfast,
Carrickfergus, Dungannon, Bandon, Clonmel, Waterford and
Limerick. These were mainly organised by two women, a Miss
Robertson of Dublin and Isabella Tod of Belfast. Isabella Tod,

Seat in St. Stephen's Green in recognition of Anne Haslam's
contribution to the Irish Suffrage Movement.

born in Scotland in 1836 of Scots-Irish parentage, later reared
in Belfast described herself as being 'of fighting stock'. In 1867
she had founded the Belfast Ladies Institute which provided
courses on the lines of similiar institutes already outlined, and
in 1873 she was the first Irishwoman to demand that women
should be admitted to Irish universities. Both women were
pioneers in spreading the suffrage doctrine in Ireland, working
chiefly through public lectures and petitions.

In 1876 Anna Haslam formed the first Irish suffrage society
in Dublin. Both she and her husband Thomas were throughout
their long lives actively engaged in many aspects of the
women's movement, and a seat in St Stephen's Green in Dublin
is dedicated to their memory. Both were quakers, Anna from
Cork, Thomas from Mountmellick, County Laois. In 1874
Thomas had published a series of pamphlets advocating
women's suffrage called *The Women's Advocate*. Only three
issues appeared, the second of which outlined methods of
political action which were to be followed by Irish suffrage
societies into the twentieth century. The leader of the English
suffrage campaign at that time, Lydia Becker, was so impressed
by this issue that she ordered five thousand copies of the
pamphlet for distribution. The Dublin Women's Suffrage
Association formed by Anna Haslam in February 1876 changed

The Women's Advocate.

"Equity knows no difference of sex. The law of equal freedom applies to the whole race—female as well as male."—HERBERT SPENCER.

No. 1.	DUBLIN.	April, 1874.

WOMEN'S SUFFRAGE.

our Metropolis that the claims of women
have not received a cordial
are manifestly just
against

The Women's Advocate.

"Equity knows no difference of sex. The law of equal freedom applies to the whole
race—female as well as male."—HERBERT SPENCER.

No. 2.

DUBLIN.

May, 1874.

except, p......
women have been som....
METHODS OF POLITICAL ACTION.
cates. Now, granting that some u..
transgressed good taste in their platform utter...
reason why our countrywomen sh....
rights ? We ...

The Women's Advocate.

"Equity knows no difference of sex. The law of equal freedom applies to the whole
race—female as well as male."—HERBERT SPENCER.

July, 1874.

DUBLIN.

No. 3.

WOMAN-SUFFRAGE *versus* "THE SPECTATOR." ...jec-
were not led astray
prejudice, we could not hesitate for
u the justice of their claim.

No doubt we hear it said that women degrade themselves by
stepping out of their natural sphere of unobtrusive modesty, and

Three issue of *The Women's Advocate,* which supported the women's suffrage movement, were published by Thomas Haslam in 1894.

its name a few times over the years, ultimately in 1901 becoming the Irish Women's Suffrage and Local Government Association (or IWSLGA, as it is referred to throughout this book).

Its membership was very small at first, and most were quakers like the Haslams. The first records of the association which have survived are for 1896, when the membership was only forty-three. By 1911 this had risen to 647, falling to 240 in 1917.[13] Great emphasis was placed on the educational role of the society, and to this end the small gatherings and meetings were organised, with well-known English and American suffragists being invited as guest speakers. In this era when communication relied on newspapers and post alone, obvious difficulties were encountered in spreading ideas to a wide audience. This was exacerbated in a country such as Ireland with few large centres of population. Committed individuals such as the Haslams and the members of their society struggled on, however. The society worked strictly by the constitutional means of petitions, public lectures, appeals to members of parliament and letters to the press. It agitated for reform of all the various legal and social measures discriminating against women, laying particular emphasis on increased educational opportunities. With the parliamentary vote as an ultimate ambition, its immediate aim was to secure for women the local government vote and women's appointment as poor law guardians. In 1838 the English Poor Law system was extended to Ireland. Boards of guardians were set up to supervise the running of workhouses established under the scheme, and to be responsible for the general operation of poor relief. Irish women who were ratepayers were entitled to vote for poor law guardians on the same conditions as men. Unlike women in England and Wales, however, they were not legally qualified to act as poor law guardians. Women householders were not entitled to the municipal franchise in Ireland – again unlike their counterparts in England – with the exception of Belfast city and the townships of Blackrock and Kingstown (Now Dún Laoghaire), where special charters applied.[14]

The IWSLGA stressed the importance of the educative role of women's involvement in public affairs. To them, attainment of these 'lesser' franchises was essential if women were to be given a chance, on the one hand to gain practical experience in public affairs, and on the other hand to prove the value of their contribution. In 1883 an act was passed which declared that canvassing and other election work could no longer be salaried. Women found they were very much in demand as unpaid party workers, particularly during elections, and women's auxiliaries of the main political parties were formed. The Primrose League (Conservative) was established in 1885, the Women's Liberal Association in 1886, and the Women's Liberal Unionist Association in 1885. Obviously it was women's usefulness rather than a desire to see them involved in politics that led to the formation of such associations. The Primrose league, for example, was always under masculine control, and the role of women in the League was essentially a social one 'acting as complements to the men'.[15] By including women in party work and using them as canvassers during elections, these organisations helped to divert attention away from the suffrage issue, and as Andrew Rosen states 'to make women feel that they were not altogether outcasts from the pole of the constitution.'[16] Significantly, between 1886 and 1892 the House of Commons did not once debate the issue of female suffrage. 1884 saw a further extension of the male franchise. Attempts at obtaining an amendment to that bill seeking a measure of suffrage for women, supported by several Irish members of parliament, failed. The Prime Minister, Gladstone opposed such an amendment on the grounds that the proposed extension of the franchise was as much as could be safely carried. Increasingly the possibility of extending the franchise to women came to be viewed in terms of party politics over and above views on the status of women. The unknown effect of a new female electorate on the fortunes of political parties caused many politicians to hesitate.

The general policy of the IWSLGA during the years 1881-94 is summarised in their report as follows:

> When any suffrage resolution or measure was before the House of Commons, letters were sent to all Irish members of Parliament urging them to support the measure. Letters

were also sent to the Irish press. explaining the bearing of the particular measure, and asking all in sympathy with it to communicate with their local Parliamantary representatives.... In 1886, twenty-seven petitions were sent to the House of Commons, and in 1890, seventeen. [17]

Despite this flurry of letters and petitions, very little was achieved until 1896, when the association was twenty years in existence. There was little if any expansion of the association during this period, and it would appear that up to 1896 the Haslams and their colleagues were preaching to the converted. A number of reasons contributed to this. Firstly, the small core of people at the heart of the IWSLGA were for many years actively involved with other issues. In addition to agitation for the Married Women's Property Acts and repeal of the Contagious Diseases Acts (which regulated prostitution), there was a series of activities in the educational field with which members of the IWSLGA were closely associated. These issues, while allied to the suffrage movement, absorbed the time and interest of the leaders, to the detriment of the suffrage campaign. Anna Haslam, in an interview in 1914, told Francis Sheehy Skeffington that the fight for repeal of the Contagious Diseases Act 'threw the suffrage movement back for ten years, we were all so absorbed in it.' [18]

Another significant factor is alluded to in the association's annual report for 1896 where we learn that no public meeting had been held since 1886 'owing to the present condition of political controversy in Ireland'. Since 1879 political activity in Ireland had focused on two main objects, the development of the Land League, and the attainment of Home Rule for Ireland. The Land League, formed by Michael Davitt in 1879, sought reform of the existing Irish land system whereby tenant farmers were forced to pay exorbitant rents to landlords, irrespective of bad harvests or poor market conditions. Resistance to evictions which occured following a concerted policy of non-payment of such rents was supported by the league, who publicised the injustices of the system, and aided those evicted. The central aim of the Land League came to be the demand for peasant proprietorship. The campaign drew enormous support from farmers, the catholic church and America, where Irish emigrants donated funds to support the cause. When the leaders of the league were arrested in 1881, the Ladies' Land League was formed by Anna Parnell to take over the work of the original league. Anna's brother, Charles Stewart Parnell was one of the arrested leaders of the league. Her sister Fanny formed a branch of the Land League in America and toured extensively to raise funds for evicted tenants. While the Ladies' Land League served the useful and essential purpose of runnng the organisation during the imprisonment of its male leaders, it was quickly squashed by Parnell on his release. Not only had the women carried on in his absence, but they had taken the initiative in re-organising the association, in many instances showing themselves more radical and determined opponents that the imprisoned leaders.[19] In addition to his involvement with the Land League, Parnell was also at this time leader of the Irish Parliamentary Party at Westminister. His quest for Home Rule looked distinctly hopeful by 1889. These hopes were quashed, however, by his involvement in a divorce case in 1890, which led to a bitter split in the Irish Party, and ultimately to his early death at the age of forty-five in 1891. The split amongst his supporters led to ten years of division within the party and in the country.

The significance of women's involvement in a national movement at this time is worth consideration. On the one hand, there was in the country an embryonic movement towards female equality, as seen in the activities of the IWSLGA. This group was mainly middle and upper class and protestant in character. On the other hand, there were women like the Parnell sisters, well aware of their disabilities as women, but who sought political change first, principally through Irish independence from England. This group were of mixed religious backgrounds and of the same classes as the IWSLGA. A similar pattern was to emerge from 1910 onwards, although by then, the issues were more clearly defined in terms of feminism versus nationalism.

In 1896 a bill was passed which allowed Irish women with certain property qualifications to serve as poor law guardians. In the House of Commons one member sought clarification of

Fanny Parnell.

the opening clause of the Bill which began 'Any female person having the qualifications which made the male person eligible...'. Mr. Gibson Bowles (MP For Lynn Regis) declared that he could not conceive that a female person could have the qualifications of a male person and went on to outline his opposition to bisexualism in public life. [20] In the House of Lords Viscount Clifden complained that he did not like to see spouting women out of their place and doing men's work, concluding that the effect of the Bill would be to largely increase the power of priests on the boards of guardians. [21] Generally however the Bill progressed smoothly through parliament. During debates in 1897 in the House of Commons on the proposed extension of the local government franchise to Irish women Henry Labouchere (MP for Northampton) referred to the first time that the issue of votes for women had been introduced into the House 30 years earlier by John Stuart Mill. He recalled that practically all MPs had viewed the suggestion as a huge joke, Mill being the only one who voted seriously. Labouchere himself, in repentance for voting with Mill then had done whatever he could since to prevent women's suffrage. He objected to petticoat government and claimed to speak for the vast majority of women who recognised that they were not fit to govern in that house, and did not wish to. His colleague Sir Barrington Simeon (MP for Southampton) declared that if ever women got into Parliament the end of the country would not be far off. [22] Despite such pessimism, the following year under the provisions of the Local Government (Ireland) Act of 1898 Irishwomen with certain property qualifications were granted the local government vote. As in England women would be entitled to sit on district councils if elected, but *not* on county councils. A proposed amendment recommending a minimum of two councillors per district (and in some cases three) was strongly supported by the IWSLGA, which claimed that this would give women some prospect of being elected to the second seat. It was stated in the House of Commons that Irish electors would elect men to represent them on questions of religion and politics but would elect women to see to the sick poor. [23] In the elections of 1899 eighty-five women were elected as poor law guardians, thirty-one of these also being elected as rural district councillors, and a further four as urban district councillors. The IWSLGA pointed out that not just those elected but also the new female electorate had participated in a significant new political experience. Like the male Home Rulers, women would later point to their competency in local government as justification for greater responsibility. The subscription list of the IWSLGA increased from this time and many of the militants of the 1912-14 period started their careers in this association.

Parallel to changes in political access for Irishwomen, other improvements in the status of women were occurring. Of particular significance was the series of improved educational facilities which occurred from the 1870s onwards, in the campaign for which the Haslams and their associates were closely involved. These included the founding of Alexandra College in Dublin in 1866 and Victoria College Belfast in 1859 and the opening of medical degrees to women in the Irish College of Physicians and Surgeons in 1877. The new girls' colleges in Dublin and Belfast aimed at cultivating the female mind along the rigorous lines hitherto preserved for boys and thus, Eibhlin Breathnach notes, inherently weakened the traditional role and image of women. Initially the impact of the new ideas was limited, the majority of protestant schools and governesses clinging to the more traditional offering of accomplishments, while the movement towards better education for girls was totally ignored in catholic circles. The Intermediate Education Act of 1878 and the Royal University Act of 1879 'caused a revolution in female education.'[24] Boys and girls now competed on equal terms in the Intermediate examinations and the degree examinations for the Royal University. At this stage some convent schools began to prepare girls for the Intermediate and University exams, mainly those under the Dominican and Loreto orders. In 1904 Trinity College Dublin – after a long hard struggle – opened its gates to women and the National University Dublin and Queens University Belfast, followed suit in 1909. These changes resulted in a body of educated articulate women impatient for reform. Many of these women were found to the fore of the various political and cultural organisations that evolved in the first two decades of the new century.

Employment opportunities were still very limited, however, with the law, civil service, accountancy and other similar professions closed. For women graduates teaching became the main occupation. The supply of teachers outstripped demand and those employed received poor wages at rates below those of their male colleagues. Nursing also suffered from problems of low pay and poor conditions, while for the majority of women the only 'career' opportunities were those notorious for exploitation such as work as shop assistants or clerks, or in low grade industrial employment or domestic service. In rural Ireland the only options were work on family farms, some poorly paid argicultural employments, or again, domestic service. There was little trade union organisation among women and little interest in working women on the part of those concerned with discrimination within the professions.

Attempts in 1903 to have poor law guardians co-opted rather than elected to relieve them from 'the worry and turmoil of a popular election'[25] forced women activists of the time to the conclusion that their existing position would not be secure until women had the parliamentary vote. The IWSLGA now set its sights firmly on attaining that goal. This it planned to do through its traditional constitutional methods. To the association, attainment of women's suffrage appeared but the next step in the evolution of the women's movement. The fact that the first steps had been attained without too much opposition, despite the long delay, may have given a false impression of future reactions. Both the poor law guardians and local government bills – while long overdue in Ireland-merely adjusted the position of Irishwomen to that of their English counterparts. Nothing new or radical was involved. It could indeed be argued that the local government vote was granted with comparative ease to women throughout the British Isles precisely because it was a limited franchise. Significantly, women were disqualfied from serving on county councils and boroughs in England and Wales until 1907, and in Ireland until 1911. The more power connected with the office, the longer it was withheld from women. Also, despite the gradual admission of women to local government boards, etc., their role on these

Cartoon from *The Irish Citizen* 1912.

NOTHING FOR THEIR "PANES."

boards was too often seen as an extension of their traditional role in the home. Thus, their advice was welcomed in matters connected with the sick poor, and in the fields of health, education and housing. When it came to matters of finance and national politics, however, they would have been encroaching on traditional male territory. With the explicit demand for parliamentary suffrage for women attitudes on both sides became tougher and more emotional. In addition, a significant new element was introduced to the struggle with the adoption by women of militant tactics. The era of the suffragette had arrived.

Cartoon from *Votes for Women*, depicting the relationship between the suffragette movement and the nationalists.

Irishwomen Unite

*It's a sure sign of the coming break-up of the planet when women
take to leaving their homes and coming out in public.* [1]

From 1900 the Irish Parliamentary Party was reunited under
the leadership of John Redmond, MP for Waterford, aided by
John Dillon. Redmond, from Wicklow, had been on Parnell's
side at the time of the split, Dillon on the opposing side. After
the general election of 1910 Redmond's party held the balance
of power at Westminister, and Home Rule for Ireland seemed
assured. Unionists (those who wished to maintain Ireland's
political union with England) strongly opposed any attempt at
establishing a separate government for Ireland.

While Redmond's party was supported by the majority of
Irish people, there had emerged in Ireland in the late
nineteenth century, a new grouping in Irish society with
broader objectives than the restoration of a native parliament. In
the years before the outbreak of World War I in 1914 the
activities of such groups had reached a peak. Their primary
ideology was one of a cultural and national renaissance, a
revival of the Gaelic language, literature. poetry, drama, folk-
lore and sports. Associations such as the Gaelic Athletic
Association (GAA) and the Gaelic League aroused the
enthusiasm of many young people, and developed in them a
sense of national identity. The Gaelic League was the most
advanced in its attitude to women, being the first association to
admit women and men on equal terms. The upsurge of interest
in things Irish and increased awareness of an historical and
cultural tradition was aided by the development of a literary
and dramatic movement, personified by poets such as WB
Yeats and AE (George Russell), dramatists such as Lady
Gregory and JM Synge, and writers such as Standish O'Grady
and James Stephens. Sinn Fein, founded in 1905 by Arthur
Griffith, provided a political outlet for many who combined the
ideal of an Irish Ireland with that of separation from England.
While Griffith advocated a policy of passive resistance – Irish
MP's should refuse to sit in Westminister and should set up an
Irish parliament in Dublin – others saw armed rebellion as the
only way to attain their objective of an Irish republic. The

various nationalist associations which had developed provided good nurturing ground for recruitment to such an ideal. From 1910 the revitalised Irish Republican Brotherhood (IRB) benefited from the rising militant spirit throughout nationalist Ireland, and was spurred on by political developments at home and abroad. In January 1913 the Ulster Volunteer Force was founded to resist by armed force the implementation of Home Rule. By the end of the year it had some 100,000 members, armed with guns and ammunition imported illegally from Europe. The IRB contemplated the establishment of a similar force in the south.

The summer of 1913, however, brought other issues to a head. Dublin at this time was a city of stark contrasts. The wealthy lived in the beautiful Georgian houses of Merrion and FilzwilliamSquares, or moved out to the growing suburbs, as train and tram services were improved. Increasingly, too, motor cars were used by the wealthy. Social life for the upper classes revolved around the centre of government administration, Dublin Castle, and around the lord lieutenant, Lord Aberdeen, and his wife. In this pre-radio and television age, newspapers were the principal source of communication, the theatre flourished and the cinema was taking hold. There was another side to life in Dublin however, that of massive unemployment. In 1913 Padraic Pearse, an early recruit to the Gaelic League, and soon to join the IRB, wrote:

> I calculate that one third of the people of Dublin are underfed; that half the children attending Irish primary schools are ill-nourished.... I suppose there are 20,000 families in Dublin in whose domestic economy milk and butter are all but unknown; black tea and dry bread are their staple diet. There are many thousand fireless hearth places in Dublin on the bitterest days of winter'. [2]

Almost one-third of Dublin's population lived in slums where over-crowding, lack of sanitation and poor diet led to disease and a high mortality rate, particularly among infants. Indeed Dublin's death rate was higher than any other city in Europe. Unlike Belfast and the major cities in Europe, Dublin

Scene outside house shows dress and housing conditions of the day.

Street scene in Dublin, 1913,
shows two young girls.

Westmoreland Street, Dublin, looking towards O'Connell Street
showing the dress and type of transport typical of the time.

had little industrial employment. Most workers were unskilled
and what work there was was mainly casual with little union
organisation and low wages.

It was these horrific conditions that men like James Larkin
and James Connolly attempted to change. Larkin, born in
Liverpool in 1876 of Irish parents, assisted by Connolly, born in
Edinburgh in 1868, also of Irish parents, organised the Irish
Transport and General Workers Union (ITGWU), and in
August 1913 direct confrontation occurred between Larkin and
the principal Dublin employers. As a result union members
were 'locked out' by employers and a bitter struggle lasting
eight months ensued. Dublin was the scene of massive
demonstrations and violence, as police and workers clashed.
The Irish Citizen Army (ICA) was formed to protect Dublin
workers from attack by the police. Both men and women could
join, and the playwright Sean O'Casey and Constance de
Markievicz, a keen supporter of Connolly, were among its

members. The ICA continued in existence after the strike and played an important role in the 1916 Rising. Shortly after the establishment of the ICA the Irish Volunteers (popularly referred to as the 'Volunteers') were formed in Dublin. There was a strong IRB element in the Volunteers. In addition, hundreds of recruits from the GAA and the Gaelic League joined, and provided many of its leaders. At their inception the Volunteers had no clear cut plan for revolution. After the outbreak of war between England and Germany in August 1914 some of the Volunteer leaders, in collaboration with Connolly and the ICA, began to formulate such plans.

In those pre-war years, therefore, Ireland was alive with movements and causes, Home Rule, Sinn Fein, Labour, the Gaelic League, all added to the melting pot that was Ireland. That melting pot also contained an active women's movement. Mary Maguire, a teacher at St Ita's, the girls' school founded by Padraic Pearse in 1910, who married the poet Padraic Colum, wrote of the period:

> Almost everything significant in the Dublin of that period was run by the young; youth, eagerness brains, imagination, are what I remember of everybody. There was something else that was in all of them: a desire for self-sacrifice, a devotion to causes; everyone was working for a cause for practically everything was a cause.... In addition to other causes I was deep in the women's suffrage movement and had read all the books about the position of women, which corresponded in a way to that of the oppressed races. [3]

Initially many young women joined the long established IWSLGA. One such woman, Hanna Sheehy Skeffington, wrote of her initiation into the suffrage movement through contact with that society:

> I was then an undergraduate, and was amazed and disgusted to learn that I was classed among criminals, infants and lunatics – in fact, that my status as a woman was worse than any of these. [4]

A Dublin woman, educated by the Dominican nuns in Eccles Street she held an MA from the Royal University and was a life-long feminist. Her father was David Sheehy, a nationalist MP from 1885 to 1918. On her marraige to Frank Skeffington in 1903 they adopted the joint name of Sheehy Skeffington. In 1904 her husband resigned his position as registrar of the Royal University over the non-recognition of women graduates.

The IWSLGA membership had been overwhelmingly non-catholic and middle class. Until then it had adopted strategies similiar to those of suffrage societies in England for attainment of its objective. With the formation of Emmeline Pankhurst's Women's Social and Political Union (WSPU) in Manchester in 1903 the concept of militant action was introduced. Emmeline and her daughters Christabel, Sylvia and Adela, were the driving force behind the new association. Christabel, soon to become the 'brain' of the organisation, had been the protégé of Eva Gore Booth (sister of Constance de Markievicz) between 1901-1904, under whom she had served her political apprenticeship in the North of England Society for Women's Suffrage (NESWS). Christabel became an executive member of the NESWS and a member of the Manchester and Salford Trade Union Council, through which she gained valuable experience in public speaking. The NESWS sought the support of working class women, and Eva Gore Booth and her co-workers held open air meetings in factory districts and spoke to women at mill gates. Another influence on the leaders of the WSPU was Charles Stewart Parnell and the tactics of the Irish Parliamentary Party. From Parnell was derived the WSPU policy of opposing all government candidates at elections – their 'keep the Government out' policy. Mrs. Pankhurst writing of the Parnellite tactics which had caused her late husband's defeat as a Liberal candidate in 1885 commented that it 'was a valuable political lesson, one that years later I was destined to put into practice'.[5] The WSPU initially depended on the Independent Labour Party for finance, publicity and audiences. This policy was later abandoned in favour of attracting wealthy donors who would not have supported a labour organisation. In Ireland the WSPU inspired emulation among young middle class women, many of them catholic, who had benefited from

Hanna Sheehy Skeffington.

the extension of higher education. In 1908 Hanna Sheehy Skeffington and Margaret Cousins, a native of Roscommon and also a graduate of the Royal University, founded the Irish Women's Franchise League (IWFL) for three main reasons: they were impatient with the IWSLGA, they admired the WSPU and they recognised the need for a separate Irish suffrage society.[6] The new society was avowedly militant but strictly 'non-party'. Its aim was to obtain the parliamentary vote for Irish women on the same terms as men then had it, or might have it. Membership was restricted to women but many men were actively involved as associates. In 1912 its membership was given at about one thousand.[7] Members of the new society realised that a women's suffrage campaign in Ireland would have to take account of current political considerations. Margaret Cousins later wrote:

> We were as keen as men on the freedom of Ireland, but we saw the men clamouring for amendments which suited their own interests, and made no recognition of the existence of women as fellow citizens. We women were convinced that anything which improved the status of women would improve, not hinder, the coming of real national self-government.[8]

The IWLF therefore worked to have a 'votes for women' clause introduced into the Home Rule for Ireland bill then under discussion.

Over the next few years a number of other smaller suffrage societies were established to cater for particular regional, religious or political groups. In 1909 an Irish branch of the Conservative and Unionist Women's Suffrage Association was established, and an independent association in Belfast named The Irish Women's Suffrage Society. By 1911, appreciating the need for co-ordination, the Irish Women's Suffrage Federation (IWSF) provided an umbrella organisation. The IWSF, established by Louie Bennett and Helen Chenevix – two Dublin women later to be active in trade union and Labour Party organisation – grew rapidly and was responsible for the formation of the Irish Women's Reform League in Dublin, and the Belfast Women's Suffrage Society. By 1913 the following societies had affiliated to the federation:

> Irish Women's Reform League, Dublin
> Belfast Women's Suffrage Society
> Munster Women's Franchise League, Cork, Skibbereen, Queenstown, Waterford, Bandon, Limerick
> Connaught Women's Franchise League, Galway
> Warrenpoint and Rostrevor Suffrage Society
> Newry Suffrage Society
> Lisburn Suffrage Society
> Nenagh Suffrage Society
> Birr Suffrage Society
> Armagh Suffrage Society
> Portrush Suffrage Society
> Bushmills Suffrage Society
> Ballymoney Suffrage Society
> Derry Suffrage Society[9]

The first president of the federation was the Hon. Mrs Spring Rice. Edith Somerville and Violet Martin, well-known authors under the pen-names of Somerville and Ross, were president and vice president respectively of the Munster women's Franchise League; they were also connected with the Conservative and Unionist Women's Suffrage Association.

In addition to its primary aim of linking together small suffrage societies scattered throughout Ireland so as to facilitate effective propaganda and educative work, the federation also hoped that such an organisation as theirs would continue to exist after attainment of the vote to carry on working for the welfare of women and of the country. The policy of the federation was to be non-party and non-militant, although some members were occasionally involved in militancy. Louie Bennett, herself strictly non-militant and a life-long pacifist, refused to condemn any women agitating for the vote, whatever method they chose. The Irish Women's Reform League (IWRL) campaigned for the provision of school meals and advocated technical education for girls. It established a lending library in Dublin specialising in books on the women's movement, and it initiated a committee to monitor legislation

Edith Somerville and Violet Martin (Somerville and Ross) in the
dining room at Drishane House.

affecting women and a 'watching the courts' committee to observe cases involving injustice to women and girls.[10]

The executive committee of the IWSF established a London committee comprising members resident in London for most of the year, who were to maintain parliamentary pressure and report on parliamentary proceedings. The IWFL also established a London branch, whose members were all of Irish birth. By May 1912 the *Irish Citizen* reckoned the total number of women suffragists at 'well over three thousand'. This mushrooming of suffrage societies reflected a changing perception by at least some women of their role in Irish society. Margaret Cousins declared proudly that 'the era of dumb, self-effacing woman was over'[11] and Hanna Sheehy Skeffington later wrote that the suffrage movement was a liberal educaton for women, bringing them forward 'for the first time in history, not for a man's cause but their own'.[12] During these years the issue of female suffrage was debated in various Irish journals and periodicals. One such article noted that 'politicians and statesmen can afford to disregard constituents who are unable to vote against them'.[13] *The Leader*, a weekly paper of the time which put forward a strong anti-English view, observed that 'the movement in Ireland smacks rather of imitation of the English, and we do not regard it as a native and spontaneous growth'.[14] The editor of that paper, D P Moran, nicknamed Irish Suffragists 'Suffs' and 'Suffers'. The catholic view was given in the *Irish Ecclesiastical Record* which stated that 'allowing woman the right of suffrage is incompatible with the catholic ideal of the unity of domestic life'. It was stated that the noise and turmoil of party politics would fare ill with the passive virtues of humility, patience, meekness, forbearance and self repression 'which are looked on by the Church as the special prerogative of the female soul'.[15]

At this time there was only one journal written for Irishwomen by Irish women. This was *Bean na hEireann*, established by Helena Molony as the journal of Inghinidhe na hÉireann, the society formed by Maud Gonne MacBride to cater for women excluded from nationalist organisations. Helena Molony, an Abbey actress, militant nationalist and trade union organiser, wrote that 'We wanted it to be a woman's paper,

advocating militancy, separatism and feminism.' In this context
the journal covered such issues as the necessity of organising
women workers in Dublin, the poor working conditions of
nurses, the migration of Irishwomen from the farm, and the
progress of the women's movement abroad. On the precise
issue of votes for Irish women and agitation to obtain franchise
'from an alien government' sharp differences arose, and the
ideal of separatism came to dominate.[16] The establishment of
the *Irish Citizen* in May 1912 provided Irish suffragists with an
essential means of communication, education and propaganda,
and incidentally, the historian with an invaluable archival
source of information on the early women's movement in
Ireland. Frank Sheehy Skeffington and James Cousins, both
married to ardent feminists, were the joint editors until 1913
when James and Margaret Cousins emigrated, first to England,
and subsequently to India. (They remained in India for the rest
of their lives, both becoming actively involved in various
aspects of Indian life, Margaret Cousins was a founder member
of the Indian Women's Association in 1917, and later she
became the first woman magistrate in India). The aim of the
paper was encompassed in its motto:

For Men and Women Equally
The Rights of Citizenship;
From Men and Women Equally
The Duties of Citizenship!

The paper was designed to cater for both militant and non-
militant suffrage workers, and from the beginning its columns
were open to contributions from all suffrage societies thus
enabling suffragists throughout the country to keep in touch
and exchange views, comments and suggestions for future
policy. Articles were published that were expressly designed to
educate Irish public opinion in the various aspects of feminism
and the struggle for women's rights, detailing the victimisation
of women workers, and highlighting the legal and social

obstacles to advancing women's status.[17]

From 1910 onwards a number of attempts to introduce a women's suffrage bill in parliament resulted from this quickening pace of activity. While many individual MPs favoured the principle of female suffrage, party consideration usually determined their attitude if a bill showed any sign of success. Liberals feared that the extension of the vote to women on the existing property basis would increase the Conservative vote. Conservatives opposed any widening of qualifications for the vote fearing increased Liberal votes. Only the Labour Party consistently supported women's suffrage proposals, while also striving to achieve its aim of general adult suffrage, i.e. suffrage for all adults, regardless of their property or lack of it. After the general election of January 1910 the Liberals no longer held a majority and the success of any legislation could no longer be achieved with the support of just one party. A committee from all political parties was organised to promote an agreed suffrage bill amenable to all. This 'conciliation committee' proposed a number of 'conciliation bills' over the next few years, all of which were unsuccessful, primarily because of party machinations. Disagreement on female suffrage was also present at cabinet level, as demonstrated in a letter from the chief secretary for Ireland, Augustine Birrell, to John Dillon, a senior member of the Irish Parliamentary Party:

> I think this active vocal split in the Cabinet on Women most serious. I don't see how I could remain in a Cabinet which has adopted en bloc Female Suffrage, married and single – and if I couldn't, how could Asquith? I believe the wire pullers are satisfied that no such Amendment can pass and that both the Conciliation Bill and the wider amendment will be lost, the one because it doesn't go far enough and the other because it goes too far. This might plainly be called trickery.[18]

The Home Rule for Ireland question, dominant in Irish and English politics, was a prime cause in hindering the progress of such bills. Some Irish MPs would have agreed with the sentiments of John Dillon to a suffrage deputation that:

Women's suffrage will, I believe, be the ruin of our
western civilisation. It will destroy the home, challenging
the headship of man, laid down by God. It may come in
your time – I hope not in mine. [19]

But others, like William Redmond (brother of the Irish party
leader) and Tom Kettle, another member of the Irish
Parliamentary Party, married to a sister of Hanna Sheehy
Skeffington's, Mary, actively supported the cause in
parliament. [20] However, when Home Rule manoeuverings
demanded they stepped into line under the leadership of John
Redmond. The Irish Parliamentary Party chief, apart from his
personal hostility to the cause, was most anxious to avoid any
issue that might adversely affect the granting of Home Rule.
The Prime Minister, Asquith, was known to be an 'anti-
suffragist'. [21]

In 1911 a new concilation bill came before parliament. Over
400 MPs had pledged themselves to vote for female suffrage,
and militancy was suspended in England to await the outcome.
Intense propaganda was carried on by suffragettes in England
and Ireland, and the lord mayor of Dublin presented a petition
in favour of the bill at the House of Commons. Concern
developed among English suffrage workers over the attitude
Irish MPs would adopt to the bill. Fears were expressed that if
the bill was successful unionists would insist on a general
election, thus endangering the imminent granting of Home
Rule. [22] Through a series of ploys the bill did not proceed as
expected, and was, in the words of Lloyd George,
'torpedoed.' [23] Militancy was renewed in England. Many
Irishwomen took part and were subsequently imprisoned in
Holloway. The *Irish Citizen* reported that thirteen IWFL
members were imprisoned in London for periods of from one
week to two months with hard labour between November 1910
and March 1912. A number of Irishwomen from other societies
were also imprisoned during this period. [24]

In 1912 the conciliation bill came up for a second reading in
parliament. The previous year this same bill had received a
majority vote of 167. This time it was defeated. The voting of
the Irish members was crucial to its defeat. Whereas in 1911

thirty-one Irish members had voted for the bill, in 1912 not one of Redmond's party voted in favour, not even those who were members of the conciliation committee. The secretary of that committee stated in a letter to the *Manchester Guardian* that the most serious single cause of the bill's defeat was the united vote of the Irish members, and that some months ago he had been warned that:

> It was necessary for the Irish Party in the interests of Home Rule to save the Liberal ministry from the disruptive effects of woman's suffrage. [25]

VOL. VI. (New Series), No. 259.   **FRIDAY, FEBRUARY** 21, 1913.   Price 1d. Weekly (Post Free 1½d.)

WHEN FOES UNITE

MR. JOHN REDMOND } "We may differ about the independence of Irish men, but we are agreed on the
MR. F. E. SMITH } subjection of Irish women."

Cartoon from *The Lepracaun* 1913.

Fears of endangering Home Rule, either by precipitating a general election or by triggering the resignation of cabinet ministers were sufficiently strong to convince all Irish members to oppose all women's suffrage measures from then on. Irish suffragists were perturbed and angry at the course of events.

Apart from heckling politicians at public meetings, militant action on the English lines of damaging property had not yet commenced in Ireland. Early in 1912 when John Redmond and his party held a meeting in the Gresham Hotel in Dublin, members of the IWFL paraded outside with banners demanding 'Home Rule for Irish Women as well as Men'. Such poster parades were a popular method of publicising one's cause in the pre-war years. Three days after the defeat of the conciliation bill in parliament, a Home Rule demonstration was held in O'Connell Street in Dublin, and the IWFL, taking advantage of the crowds in the city for the occasion, organised another poster parade. As the women's march ended there occured what the *Freeman's Journal*, a Dublin newspaper, described as 'some unpleasant incidents' during which the women's group was treated roughly by stewards, and had their posters forcibly taken from them and torn up.[26] The stewards were reputedly members of the Ancient Order of Hibernians, a sectarian catholic organisation which supported the Irish Parliamentary Party. Later in 1912 John Redmond received a deputation from the IWFL, and it became known that he refused to support female suffrage either in the Home Rule bill or after Home Rule was established.[27] Apart from his personal views on the suffrage issue, Redmond, like Carson, undoubtedly feared the effects on his party of a vastly increased electorate. The IWFL declared war on the Irish party. When the Irish Home Rule bill was introduced in the House of Commons in April 1912, not surprisingly, it contained no reference to female suffrage, and Irish members were subsequently responsible for the defeat of a number of proposed women's suffrage amendments to the bill. The Home Rule bill was bitterly opposed by the WSPU which organised a poster parade outside the Houses of Parliament proclaiming 'No votes for Women, No Home Rule'. John Redmond organised a national convention in Dublin in April 1912 to consider the Bill. Women

Cartoon from *The Lepracaun* 1912.

were excluded. Tom Kettle failed to keep his promise to move a resolution favouring the extension of votes to women under the new government. A mass meeting of Irish women was held in Dublin in June 1912 to demand the inclusion of female suffrage in the Home Rule Bill.[28] The following societies were represented: the IWFL, Dublin and Limerick; the IWSS, Belfast, Bangor and Derry; the IWSF, and the following constituent societies – IWRL, Dublin, MWFL, Cork and Waterford; Belfast Women's (non-militant) Suffrage Society; suffrage societies of Lisburn, Armagh, Newry, Warrenpoint, Birr; Ighinidhe na hEireann; the IWWU; the Ladies Committee of the Irish Drapers' Assistants' Association. Delegates also attended from counties Tipperary, Galway, Mayo, Wicklow, Sligo, Westmeath, Clare, Roscommon, Kilkenny, Kerry, Louth and Wexford. Representatives from suffrage societies throughout Ireland were joined by women trade unionists and nationalist women. Constance de Markievicz, daughter of the aristocracy turned republican and keen supporter of the labour movement, Kathleen Lynn, medical doctor, suffrage supporter and nationalist, Jennie Wyse Power, a suffragist who had in her youth been a member of the Ladies' Land League, and who was at this time vice-president of Sinn Fein, Delia Larkin, first secretary of the IWWU formed in 1911, and sister of James Larkin and Helen Chenevix were among those on the platform. Messages of support were received from many individuals and organisations, including James Connolly, Maud Gonne MacBride, George Russell, William Sears, editor of the *Enniscorthy Echo* and keen supporter of women's rights, Helena Moloney and Louie Bennett. Mary Hayden, professor of modern Irish history at University College Dublin, chaired the meeting. The unity of feeling experienced by women from radically different political backgrounds is evident from the speeches given and messages received.[29] So we find a Belfast woman stating:

> I write from the purely Unionist point of view. But it seems to me imperative that all women, of whatever political party, should now stand for a great principle – the principle that no democratic Government can be considered complete which ignores not only a class but a whole sex.

Likewise Jennie Wyse Power, vice-president of Sinn Fein stated:

> I commend this meeting to the men of Ireland as an example. This is the first united demand from the Irish People on the proposal to change the constitution of the country. The Sinn Fein Party, to which I belong, passed unanimously a resolution in favour of votes for women, and as an Irish Nationalist I cannot see why there should be any antagonism between the Irish women's demand for citizenship and the demand for a native Parliament. Our claim is that we shall not be debarred merely by sex from the rights of citizens.

The position of women at that time was encapsulated in the remarks of another northern speaker:

> Whatever may happen in Ireland, Suffragists realise that

under the Home Rule Bill, as it at present stands, one half of the responsible population of the country will continue to be governed by the other half.

The meeting unanimously adopted the following resolution:

That while expressing no opinion on the general question of Home Rule, this Mass Meeting of Delegates from the Irish Suffrage Societies and other women's organisations representing all shades of political and religious opinion, profoundly regrets the proposal to establish a new Constitution in Ireland on a purely male franchise, and calls upon the Government to amend the Home Rule Bill in Committee by adopting the Local Government Register (which includes women) as the basis for the new parliament.

Copies of the resolution were sent to each cabinet member and to all Irish MPs. It was ignored by all. The IWFL decided to initiate militancy in Ireland.[30]

Jenny Wyse Power.

MEMORIAL

To His Excellency The Earl of Aberdeen KT.

Lord Lieutenant of Ireland

We, the Undersigned beg most respectfully to appeal to your Excellency upon behalf of the four Dublin Suffragette Prisoners, Maud Lloyd, Hilda Webb, Marjorie Hasler, and Kathleen Houston, at present undergoing sentences of six months imprisonment in Mountjoy Prison for breaking panes of glass in the windows of certain Government Offices in this city, in the hope that your Excellency may see your way to exercise your prerogative and grant a remission of the remaining portion of the sentences imposed upon the aforesaid Prisoners.

Your Memorialists beg to refer your Excellency to the fact that the offence for which these ladies have been imprisoned was committed concurrently with, and was similar to, that for which four other Dublin ladies received sentences of one month's imprisonment, with an additional month in default of giving Bail.

The Prisoners upon whose behalf we now appeal to your Excellency have been confined in prison since the 12th day of July last, and are now entering upon the sixteenth week of their sentences, which will not expire till the 12th day of December next.

Trusting your Excellency may see your way to accede to the request of your Memorialists,

We beg to subscribe ourselves,

Your Excellency's obedient Servants,

[handwritten signatures]

Following the conviction of eight women for glass breaking, nine of the Jury submitted this memorial to the lord lieutenant seeking a remission of the sentence.

Action and Reaction

The first stone was flung in 1912 when Irishwomen were excluded from the vote in the Home Rule Bill.... As a protest, the Irish Women's Franchise League followed a careful plan...women in the early morning hours, having originally selected their buildings, taking sticks along, smashed quite a goodly number of panes of glass in Government buildings, in the GPO, the Custom House, Dublin Castle'.[1]

On 13 June 1912 eight members of the IWFL were arrested for breaking the windows of government buildings in Dublin. The occurrence excited dramatic headlines and editorial condemnation in the Dublin press. The *Irish Times* expressed its abhorrence of the incident proclaiming 'the persons responsible for this outrage have dragged the name not only of Irish suffragists, but of the whole Irish public in the dust'.[2] The *Irish Citizen* defended the militant action stating:

> It would be ludicrous, were it not shameful, to find nationalists, whose history is a record of success gained by the use of violence and lawbreaking and damage to property, condemning the smashing of a few panes of glass as if it were an unheard of and unpardonable outrage, or to find Unionists, while vehemently applauding the resolve of Ulster to resist Home Rule by illegal methods, and encouraging them to drill for the purpose of armed resistance, at the same time condemning last Thursday's window-smashing in the name of Irish reputation for sanity and sobriety in the conduct of their social and political affairs.[3]

The women were sentenced and fined according to the amount of damage they had caused. All refused to pay fines or accept bail. One group of four served two months imprisonment, the remaining four served almost five of their six months sentence. In November 1912 a memorial to the lord lieutenant on behalf of the latter group seeking remission of the remainder of their sentence, was signed by nine of the jury which had convicted them, including the jury foreman.[4] Hanna Sheehy Skeffington, one of those imprisoned, related in her memoirs how one meal a day was sent to the prison for the women from Jennie Wyse Power's restaurant in Henry Street, Dublin. Her husband Frank, who visited her every day, was advised by the prison governor to persuade Hanna to be 'sensible'. Her son Owen, then aged three, was once allowed to visit her in her cell – an unheard of concession – because he had fallen on the stone floor of the reception room and raised such a howl that the superintendent feared if he went out howling, it might be reported in the press.

The British Prime Minister, Asquith, was due to visit Dublin on 18 July 1912 in connection with the Home Rule bill. He categorically refused to receive deputations from any type of suffrage society during his visit. Some weeks earlier he had stated the he would consider it a calamity if any system of Irish self-government were implemented which excluded from participation in the affairs of the country any section of Irish opinion and of Irish interest.[5] Where, one wonders, did he place the female half of the Irish people? Similarly, when John Dillon rejected the proposal for the exclusion of Ulster from the Home Rule bill stating 'It must be Home Rule for all, or none at all', the *Irish Citizen* pointed out that 'Home Rule for all means "Home Rule for Men".' For days before the Asquith visit inflammatory letters were published in the Dublin evening papers threatening suffragettes if they attempted any demonstrations during his visit. Most of these letters were signed with pen-names, 'Home-Ruler' being the most popular. One such letter warned Frank Sheehy Skeffington that 'should he and his suffragist friends begin their dirty tricks and surprises, they may expect to receive at the hands of Nationalists more than what they bargained for'.[6]

Another writer suggested that the police should 'use whips on the shoulders of those unsexed viragoes...slender, springy, stinging riding whips'.[7] Newspaper editorials also warned against any suffrage demonstrations during the Asquith visit, although not in quite such colourful terms. The *Evening Telegraph* warned:

Any attempt to interfere with the Prime Minister during his visit here will be accepted as a declaration of war on the Home Rule movement. Mr Sheehy Skeffington and the little band who share his views had better keep their hands off Mr Asquith. [8]

As events turned out these threats were taken seriously – and almost literally – by a section of Irish nationalists. A number of demonstrations were staged by Irish suffragettes during the Asquith visit. One of these involved a party of women who went out in a small boat near Asquith's boat at Kingstown (now Dun Laoghaire) Co. Dublin with 'Votes for Women' placards, and a megaphone through which they directed to the prime minister appeals for the inclusion of women in the Home Rule bill. The focal point of the visit was to be a big Home Rule gathering in the Theatre Royal at which Asquith and John Redmond would speak. Entry to this meeting was by ticket only, applications for which were carefully vetted. Despite stringent precautions, Frank Sheehy Skeffington managed to get a ticket and gain entry disguised as a clergyman. His plan was to interrupt Mr Asquith at a relevant point in his speech with a question regarding the inclusion of women in the bill. This he did and, as expected, he was unceremoniously ejected from the hall. [9]

Apart from one instance of window-breaking by a member of the IWFL, the militant demonstrations carried out were rather tame. In addition to the boat and heckling incidents, the IWFL organised poster parades and a public protest meeting to be held simultaneously with the Asquith meeting. The non-militants sent a petition to Mr Asquith, which he refused to receive in person.

Whatever chance there might have been of the visit and demonstrations passing off without incident was unexpectedly shattered by the actions of three English members of the WSPU who had travelled to Dublin for the Asquith visit unknown to Irish suffragettes. The first incident in which these women were involved was the throwing of a hatchet into the carriage in which Asquith and John Redmond were travelling. The hatchet missed Asquith but Redmond was slightly grazed on the ear.

Newspaper headlines denounced 'The Virago and the Hatchet' and the 'Hatchet Outrage'. [10] The idea of a woman attacking the prime minister with a hatchet while he was surrounded by dignatories and police may seem far-fetched, but the police had received information that an attack would be made on Asquith as he rode through Dublin. A confidential report sent to the chiefs of police and the chief secretary stated:

> There is a plot on foot to assassinate the Prime Minister on the occasion of his visit to Dublin on 19th instant. The instigators of the plot are the advanced section of the militant Suffragists. The attack is to be made while Mr Asquith is driving through the city from the railway station on his arrival, and will come from a house. In order to guard against failure the horses are to be shot first, and then when the carraige has thus been brought to a stand-still, several shots are to be fired at Mr Asquith. [11]

The second incident in which the Englishwomen were involved was an arson attempt at the Theatre Royal in the city centre where Asquith was to speak. The day before the meeting one of the women set fire to the curtains in one of the boxes. It was quickly noticed, however, and extinguished. There followed within minutes an explosion inside the theatre, also caused by the women. Due to the prompt action of some patrons still in the theatre very little damage was caused. The Englishwomen were arrested and an examination of their lodgings revealed explosives. They were remanded in custody and sent for trial.

Again newspapers were provided with much headline material, and decried the 'Reign of Terror' and 'Dastardly Outrage'. [12] The *Evening Telegraph* headline read 'Ladies who have no religion – only Votes for Women', this being the answer given by one of the women to prison officials. The IWFL immediately denied all knowledge of the presence of English Suffragettes in Dublin stating that the league had no association with English suffrage groups beyond unity of demand. Non-militant societies also dissociated themselves from the militant acts, while the Munster Women's Franchise League expressed

Mary had a little bag,
  And in it was a hammer,
For Mary was a suffragette,
  For votes she used to clamour.
She broke a pane of glass one day,
  Like any naughty boy,
A constable came along,
  And now she's in Mountjoy.

Cartoon from *The Lepracaun,* November 1912.

its 'abhorrence of the wicked actions of the English suffragettes'. One of the signatories to this statement was Mary McSwiney, later to be involved in controversy between suffragists and nationalists. In spite of these protestations the immediate effect of these incidents was that all suffragists in Dublin, irrespective of method or nationality, were suspect and for a time became the objects of mob-violence. The IWFL had organised an open-air meeting at Beresford Place adjacent to Liberty Hall, headquarters of the Irish Transport and General Workers Union (ITGWU), to coincide with the Asquith meeting in the Theatre Royal, a short distance away. As they started their meeting a large hostile crowd assembled, which was later augumented by crowds who had been cheering Asquith on his arrival at the theatre. There developed what the *Irish Independent* described as 'trouble of a very serious nature'.[13] The women on the IWFL platform were heckled with shouts of 'down with the suffragettes', 'we will never forget the hatchet', 'burn them', 'throw them in the river'. The crowd became so hostile that police had to form a barrier between them and the speakers' stand. A police inspector later testified in court that after half an hour he advised the women involved against continuing the meeting, and the women were escorted by about fifty policemen to O'Connell Street. The police were forced to draw batons a number of times along the way, particularly in Abbey Street where the crowd became particularly menacing with cries of 'let us get at them and we'll give them what they deserve'. On reaching O'Connell Street the crowd had increased to one thousand according to the *Irish Independent*, and the police again had to draw their batons. They finally succeeded in getting the party of women on board a Rathmines tram, and it left with a police escort amid breaking glass as the crowd broke some of its windows.

Within minutes it was discovered that another suffragette was in trouble. A furious mob was on the point of carrying out the advice offered in the letters column of the *Evening Telegraph*, i.e. that suffragettes should be thrown into the Liffey. Luckily the police rescued her in time. Further mobbing of women occurred at Eden Quay, the victims this time including Constance de Markievicz. Once again a large force of police came to the rescue and, not without difficulty, escorted them to a tram, which was followed for some distance by a booing and threatening crowd. Constance de Markievicz took shelter in Liberty Hall, and in so doing was roughly handled by the crowd. Another nationalist woman invovled in the suffragette movement – Jennie Wyse Power – had her home surrounded by a hostile mob. Numerous incidents of violence and threats against women occurred that day and these were not reserved for known suffragettes. The *Irish Independent* reported that 'Every woman respectably dressed went in danger of being singled out by the mob as a suffragette, and a state of panic prevailed.' The paper reported cases where women's clothes were almost torn from them before the police could reach them. Katherine Tynan, Dublin poet and novelist, describing the events of that night wrote that 'the women were hunted like rats in the city'.[14] For about two weeks after these incidents suffrage meetings of all societies were attended by organised hooliganism. The *Irish Citizen* was not alone in condemning such conduct. The *Irish Independent* editorial, championing the right of women to air their views stated... 'it is certainly not in keeping with our traditional courtesy towards women to find their meetings interrupted and broken up by apparently organised gangs of men and youths'.[15] The *Leader* also defended women's right to free speech stating that 'these people, however eccentric they may be, are entitled to advocate votes for women in public...they should not be treated to physical violence.'[16] The Sinn Fein journal was also highly critical of the mob, while its national council adopted a resolution condemning as 'un-Irish and unmanly the forcible interference with the right of any section of Irishwomen to publicly claim the suffrage'.

At this time, when the popularity of the IWFL was at a low ebb, James Connolly demonstrated his support for the women's movement by travelling from Belfast to speak at the weekly public meeting of the league, an action long and greatly appreciated by the women. Also, members of his union, the ITGWU, often protected suffragettes at their meetings.[17] Pressure of public opinion, as demonstrated through newspaper editorials and letters, combined with police activity and arrests eventually brought an end to this violence.

Meanwhile, the trial of the English suffragettes proceeded.[18] The charge of throwing a hatchet into Asquith's carriage was dropped on the second day of the trial. The *Irish Citizen* claimed that this was due to Redmond's reluctance to appear as a witness. There were precedents for politicians not proceeding with charges against suffragettes. The chief secretary for Ireland, Augustine Birrell, after being slightly injured in a fracas with suffragettes in Downing Street in London, declined to prosecute, but wrote to Winston Churchill 'let the matter drop but keep your eyes on the hags in question'.[19] Two of the wo nen – Mary Leigh and Gladys Evans – were sentenced to five years penal servitude, while the third – Lizzie Baker was sentenced to seven months hard labour. There was an immediate outcry from English and Irish suffrage groups at the severity of the sentences. Christabel Pankhurst, one of the leaders of the WSPU, wrote that 'even they [the government] realise that women cannot be sent for five years to convict prisons as an alternative to giving them the vote.'[20] In an editorial on the sentences *Sinn Fein* condemned the English women for perpetrating such acts in Ireland declaring that 'Irish women suffragists have not yet realised that the English woman in politics is as much an exploiter of Irish women as the

Police District of Dublin⎫
Metropolis, to wit. ⎭   **Form A.** SOUTHERN DIVISION.

To the Keeper of Mountjoy Prison, Kilmainham Gaol, a place of imprisonment in said District,

WHEREAS Hannah Sheehy Skeffington a Prisoner herewith sent, is this day duly Convicted upon oath before Me the undersigned, one of the Divisional Justices of said district, presiding at the Dublin Metropolitan Police Court, Inns Quay in said District, of having on the 13 day of June 190 2 at Ship St Barracks in said district wilfully damaged to the extent of £ 11 0 19 panes of glass, property of the war Department

contrary to the

Statute in that case made and provided, and I, the said Justice, thereupon adjudge the said Prisoner, for said Offence, to forfeit and pay the Sum of Forty Shillings and ⎯ Pence for Penalty, and in default of the immediate payment of said Penalty, to be imprisoned in the said place of imprisonment for the space of one cal. month.

with

AND WHEREAS the said Prisoner has failed to pay the said Penalty.

THEREFORE, you are now hereby required to receive into your custody and safely keep, as I have adjudged as aforesaid the body of the said Prisoner, for the said period of imprisonment from the date hereof,

unless the said Penalty shall be sooner paid, and being satisfied that there is danger of a future breach of the peace by said prisoner, I further order that the said Prisoner shall be bound to keep the Peace and be of good behaviour towards the said all His Majesty's liege subjects for Twelve Months, her self in £ 10 and two surety in £ 10 each, and in default thereof that from the expiration of the last mentioned period of imprisonment or payment of the last mentioned penalty which ever first shall happen the said prisoner be further Imprisoned in said place of imprisonment for one cal month. And for so doing this shall be your sufficient Warrant.

Given under my Hand and Seal, this 20 day of June 190 2.
(Sigd.) E. G. Swiffte. (SEAL)
One of the said Justices

A true copy
C. J. Brien Lewis 20 Bees
Governor.   Inspr. Queens.

Notice from Dublin Metropolitan Police, dated 13 June 1912, to the keeper of Mountjoy Prison, committing Hanna Sheehy Skeffington for one month.

Englishman in politics is an exploiter of Irish men'.[21] Jennie Wyse Power, then vice-president of Sinn Fein, deploring the attitude of the editorial, wrote in reply that Irish people with memories of agitation should be slow to blame women who have been goaded into revolution by government tactics, asking 'may one who had suffered suggest to all Irish men to realise that this is a woman's question'[22]

This exchange articulated differences which were to emerge again in the relationship between suffragists and nationalists. Having been refused recognition as political prisoners the English suffragettes went on hunger strike on 14 August 1912. The following day four of the Irish suffragettes also in Mountjoy jail went on hunger-strike in sympathy with the

Prison document from Mountjoy Prison relating to Hanna Sheehy Skeffington.

Englishwomen. Hanna Sheehy Skeffington later wrote 'Hunger-strike was then a new weapon – we were the first to try it out in Ireland – had we but known, we were the pioneers in a long line'.[23] The Irish suffragettes were not forcibly fed, and remained on hunger-strike until the termination of their sentence five days later. While one English prisoner – Lizzie Baker, serving seven months – was released on health grounds, the other two were forcibly fed from 20 August, six days after they had commenced their hunger-strike. The introduction of forcible feeding into Ireland met with much public disapproval, demonstrated in the letters and petitions which poured into the Chief Secretary's office. Despite such protests forcible feeding of the two women continued. The chief secretary, Augustine

Birrell, in a letter to John Dillon, outlined his views on forcible
feeding:

> Personally I am dead against Forcible Feeding which
> always ends with the release of the prisoner long before
> her time. I want to keep these ladies under lock and key
> for five years and I am quite willing to feed them with
> Priests Champagne and Michaelmas Geese all the time, if
> it can be done but...these wretched hags...are obstinate to
> the point of death.[24]

A WSPU representative who visited Dublin during this
period voiced fears that the authorities planned to place Mary
Leigh in a mental asylum because of their constant references to
her being mad. An interesting light is shed on this notion by
prison-board records which show that should the women have
been temporarily released and subsequently recommitted to
prison, it was proposed to transfer them to Tullamore female
prison, to locate them in the prison hospital and to 'treat them
from the start as Hospital patients (borderline insane cases)'.[25]
Eventually both women were released on convict licence and
hospitalised – Mary Leigh having been forcibly fed for forty-six
days and Gladys Evans for fifty-eight days.[26]

Between 1912 and the outbreak of war in August 1914 there
were thirty-five convictions of women in Ireland for suffrage
activities. Twenty-two of these incidents took place in Dublin,
mostly involving damage to government property.[27] Although
a total of twelve suffrage prisoners went on hunger-strike in
Irish prisons during these years, only in the case of Leigh and
Evans was forcible feeding used. In England, with much larger
numbers of suffrage prisoners, forcible feeding had been used
extensively, and the resulting public outcry forced the
government to seek another solution to the problem. In the
spring of 1913 a bill was introduced to allow for the temporary
release of hunger-strikers when their health was endangered,
until they were fit enough to be recommitted. Their period of
release would not count as part of the sentence. As
reimprisoned women usually recommenced their hunger-
strike immediately, under the terms of the bill sentences of a

few months could be spread over an indefinite period. The bill, officially termed 'The Prisoners (Temporary Discharge for Ill Health) Bill', became popularly known as the 'Cat and Mouse Act'. On 25 April this bill became law, with the support of the Irish Parliamentary Party. This action was consistent with the attitude of the party some weeks earlier, when sixty-two Irish MPs took part in a vote of confidence in the government's policy of forcible feeding.[28] The only Irish member to oppose the act was TM Healy, a member of the Irish Parliamentary Party since the Parnell days. Although forcible feeding was suspended after the final ratification of the Act on 25 April 1913, it was reverted to later that year, due to difficulties in re-arresting prisoners, and to their involvement in illegal activities while free on licence. When an attempt was made to implement the Cat and Mouse Act in Ireland in June 1913, widespread protest meetings and petitions were organised. Among those

PRISONERS (TEMPORARY DISCHARGE FOR ILL-HEALTH) ACT, 1913.

NOTICE TO BE GIVEN TO PRISONER.

Marguerette Palmer is this day discharged from Tullamore Prison in pursuance of the Lord Lieutenant's Order of the 17th June 1913, subject to the following conditions:

1. The prisoner shall return to the above-mentioned prison on the second day of July, 1913

2. The period of temporary discharge granted by this Order may, if the Lord Lieutenant thinks fit, be extended on a representation by the prisoner that the state of her health renders her unfit to return to prison. If such representation be made, the prisoner shall submit her-self, if so required, for medical examination by the Medical Officer of the above-mentioned Prison or other registered medical practitioner appointed by the Lord Lieutenant.

3. The prisoner shall notify the place of residence to which she goes on her discharge to the Chief Officer of Police of the district in which such residence is situated. The prisoner shall not change her residence without giving one clear day's previous notice in writing to the said Chief Officer of Police, specifying the residence to which she is going, and she shall not be temporarily absent from her residence for more than twelve hours without giving a like notice.

4. The prisoner shall abstain from any violation of the law.

If she fails to comply with any of the foregoing conditions, the prisoner is liable to be arrested and taken back to prison. While she is at large under this Order the currency of her sentence is suspended.

(Sd.) J. Boland
Governor.

18th June 1913.

Document authorising the release of Marguerette Palmer under The Cat and Mouse Act, signed by J. Boland, Governor.

Marguerette Palmer.

who gave their support to these protests were Constance de Markievicz, Professor Tom Kettle and Padraic Pearse, teacher, poet and one of the leaders of the 1916 rebellion. Speaking at one such protest meeting in the Mansion House in Dublin, Tom Kettle stated that he was prepared not to sacrifice, but to postpone, any social or franchise reform for the sake of seeing Ireland mistress in her own household. This was greeted with cries of 'you're not a woman' and 'that's not the women's view'.[29] The provisions of the Cat and Mouse Act were not applied, and the *Irish Citizen* claimed this to be a major triumph due largely to the support of Irish public opinion.

By the end of 1912 suffrage societies in Ireland were more numerous and more widespread that ever before. The columns of the *Irish Citizen* reported the increasing number of societies, and the extensive range of propaganda devices used in the campaign[30] At this stage the number of societies and branches had risen from fifteen in November 1912 to twenty-nine in May 1913. Hanna Sheehy Skeffington later wrote:

> We held parades, processions, pageants (a Pageant of
> Great Women which went back to Irish history for
> heroines).... We had colours (orange and green), a Votes
> for Women badge, slogans; we made use with feminine
> ingenuity of many good publicity devices and stunts...and
> became a picturesque element in Irish life.... Women
> speakers who could hold their own,... meeting heckling
> on their own ground, being good-humoured and capable
> of keeping their temper under bombardments of rotten
> eggs, over-ripe tomatoes, bags of flour, stinking chemicals,
> gradually earned respect and due attention: Suffs were
> good sports.

Prominent English suffragettes such as Sylvia Pankhurst, sister of Christabel, and Charlotte Despard, formerly a member of the WSPU, but from 1907 president of a breakaway organisation, The Women's Freedon League, visited Ireland and addressed public meetings. Charlotte Despard's brother – Lord French – was lord lieutenant of Ireland from 1918 to 1921. When women were imprisoned, intensive publicity was attained by colleagues through public meetings, the organising of petitions and other means. In addition the prisoners themselves maintained pressure within the prison through insistence on their rights as political prisoners, threatening and resorting to hunger-strike in a number of instances. The fact that suffragettes were prepared to go to prison, and to hunger-strike if necessary, won some popular approval. Margaret Cousins writing of her arrival with two other suffragette prisoners at Tullamore railway station en route to that town's jail informs us:

> To our surprise, all the casual visitors at the railway
> station, all the station porters, car drivers, newsboys,
> formed a procession of sympathy behind us, and our
> police guard, and escorted us the short distance on foot
> from the station to the big feudal-looking Tullamore jail,
> and gave us a cheer as we entered its fear-evoking gate.[31]

The women went on hunger-strike for six days in support of their demand for political prisoner status. When their demands were met and the strike was called off, Margaret Cousins reports that the chairman of the town council came to visit her 'bringing a soft down pillow'. The IWFL reported constant activity by league members in Tullamore during the imprisonment, and that Tullamore urban council passed a unanimous resolution demanding political treatment for the women.

Not all their experiences were quite so heartwarming, however. When the IWFL toured Roscommon a great deal of hostility was encountered. Hanna Sheehy Skefffington

Tullamore prisoners:
Margaret Cousins,
Margaret Connery,
Barbara Hoskins, Mabel
Purser.

reported that the crowd in Boyle threatened to throw them in the river, and stoned their hotel, informing a local priest that 'they hadn't had such fun since the Parnell split'.[32] In July 1912, Monsignor Keller of Youghal, speaking to convent school pupils, attacked the suffragettes as

> ...that strange tribe, small in number, that has arisen on the horizon in Ireland in quite recent times.... They are not men, they are not women. Woman: the idea comprises dignity, self-respect, refinement, reserve. I don't find any of these qualities among the Suffragettes.[33]

Hanna Sheehy Skeffington in her memoirs stated that generally the press, Sinn Fein and the clergy were opposed to the militant campaign, even though the women's violence was mostly symbolic. Noting that in Ireland, as in agricultural communities generally, there is a strong prejudice against women working on independent lines, she instances cases of clerical opposition to 'this insidious enemy of the home', sometimes so effective that women could not hold a public meeting in a town.[34] The catholic clergy were not unique in denigrating the women's suffrage movement. The (Church of Ireland) dean of St Patrick's Cathedral in Dublin, the Very Reverend C T Ovenden, refused permission for a service to be held for suffragette prisoners, and the *Church of Ireland Gazette* in 1914 advocated deportation for militant suffragettes.[35] The student magazine of University College Dublin, both as *St Stephen's* and *The National Student* was not in favour of the suffrage movement. In reporting debates on the subject, editorial support was invariably given to those opposing the motion. An article in 1914 on what the word 'liberty' meant to intellectuals stated that among other things, the word meant votes for women, 'with its usual corollary of easily obtained divorce'. In 1912, the periodical the *Catholic Bulletin* printed a story on the theme of women's suffrage. 'Kitty's fight for Freedom' told the story of a young girl enticed into the suffrage movement by 'a spinster of uncertain age...thin and hatchet-faced'. Her fiancé 'belonged to the type of man who believes that women are made to be cherished and shielded from contact with a rough world...his was essentially a masculine

AN OPEN LETTER TO THE BISHOP OF ROSS.

[Most Rev. Dr. Kelly, Bishop of Ross, in his Lenten Pastoral, refers to the effort of womankind to escape from dependence on man, aping his dress, copying his social habits, and displacing him in most callings, except in the trenches and fighting line, and on board the Dreadnoughts. " Many women," he says, " bitten by the Higher Education craze, openly and aggressively assert their own superiority, and, reversing God's order, attempt to exercise dominion over men."]

I am exceedingly glad I don't live in your diocese, because I earn my living doing a man's work for a third of his pay, and living, too, what no doubt your Lordship would consider an idle life—**for a woman.** Going out to work very day, as I do, I know a good deal about the standards of work, conduct and appearance exacted from the weaker sex for much less wage than is considered barely enough for the lords of creation.   It is perfectly true that I do not need the surplus required by your lordship's sex to expend on drink, tobacco, or immorality.   All the same, I own I do like to dress neatly and, if I could afford it, daintily, but I need not tell you **my** stipend does not run to the laces and silks your lordship flaunts in.   I own, too, I like to have a bit of ready money to save a woman from coming within the sphere of the patronage of your Lordship's sex.   No doubt your holiness knows as well as I do, remote as your pastoral indicates you are from real life, the payment exacted.

I find my life a fairly hard one, on the whole, but I have at least the consolation of not coming within the sphere of your Lordship's spiritual ministrations, and so I can keep my religion and conduct free from the fog of sex-prejudice that hangs over Lordship's pastoral, and can subscribe myself—   **A Working Woman.**

Letter published in *The Irish Citizen* 1913.

chivalrous nature.' After taking part in a suffrage demonstration, meeting a hostile reception and rough treatment by the crowd, Kitty is rescued by her fiance, the engagement is restored, and the story ends with the blushing heroine telling her suffragette friend that 'it is much more satisfactory to have a man do these disagreeable things for one.'

In September 1913 the English WSPU started a campaign in Ulster to obtain from Sir Edward Carson, leader of the Ulster unionists, the assurance of an equal share for women in his planned provisional government.[36] The WPSU also established a Dublin branch. Among the reasons given for this move by Christabel Pankhurst to Hanna Sheehy Skeffington were the facts that 'John Redmond is to so large an extent the arbiter of the fate of English women', and that 'the Nationalist members hold the fate of the Suffrage Cause for the whole kingdom in their hands.'[37] The *Irish Citizen* agreed that pressure should be placed on Carson, but preferred that such a task should be undertaken by native Irish societies. Its editorials suggested that perhaps Ulster suffrage groups had not been sufficiently active in this regard, and had left the field open for WSPU intervention. While up to this time all Irish suffragette militancy had occurred in Dublin, from late in 1913 the majority of militant acts occured in Ulster. These differed from the Dublin campaign in attacking private rather than government property, and increased in tempo parallel with the arson campaign of the WSPU in England. In March 1914 a group of WSPU activists laid seige to Sir Edward Carson's London home for four days. When Sir Edward eventually consented to receive a deputation he informed the women that his leadership of the Ulster party made him only responsible for opposing Home Rule, that he and his Ulster unionist colleagues were not of one mind on the issue of parliamentary votes for women, and that he had no intention of introducing dissension into his party. The WSPU responded by declaring war on him and his party, and commenced a campaign of arson in Ulster. Shortly afterwards a mansion, in the grounds of which Ulster unionists had been holding military drills, was destroyed by fire. There followed a series of arson attacks in the province.[38] When the government announced its offer to militant Ulster unionists, namely the exclusion from the Home Rule bill of such counties of Ulster as might declare by referendum that they wanted to be excluded, northern suffragists pointed accusingly to the contrast between this recognition of the efficacy of Sir Edward Carson's militant campaign, and the persistent refusal of the government to concede anything to the militant women.

The WPSU newspaper, *The Suffragette*, was particularly scathing about the contrast in treatment of militant men and women in the north. In April 1914 the WPSU offices in Belfast were raided by police, and the women were arrested on charges of possessing explosives. This was described by the *Irish Citizen* as a 'ludicrous charge in view of the notorious accumulation of explosives and other war-munitions in Belfast by men.' Government records show strong disapproval by sections of the northern public of the action of militant suffragettes. When a bomb exploded in Lisburn protestant cathedral, four women were arrested in connection with the incident. The crown solicitor, reporting his investigations to the attorney general, wrote that:

> The news of the explosion at that early hour awakened the whole town of Lisburn, and knowing the accused, Mrs Metge, to be a militant suffragette, some time later on in the morning a crowd made an attack upon her house breaking all the windows and bespattering the house with mud. The County Inspector informed me that the rabble had treatened to lynch her as she came back to Lisburn, and he was of the opinion that it would be difficult for him to protect her even with a large increase of the police under his control.[39]

Between March and August 1914, thirteen women were arrested for militant activity in the north. Meanwhile, suffrage violence had almost ceased in Dublin. Why had the IWFL abandoned its policy of militant action? With one exception, all militant acts in Dublin had taken place in direct response to current parliamentary developments on women's suffrage, and most referred specifically to the role of the Irish Party in such developments. From May 1913 no new developments

Mrs Metge, Belfast.

Mrs Margaret Connery with Edward Carson and John
Redmond during a protest over the Bonor Laws.

occurred. Interest centered mainly on the attitudes and actions of Ulster unionists *vis-a-vis* impending Home Rule. It is likely that the IWFL deliberately abstained from militant action during this period rather than be associated with northern arsonists. Coincidentally, the rising spirit of militarism in 1914, manifested in England by rumblings of war, in Ireland by the activities of the Ulster Volunteers and the Irish Volunteers, gave pause to some Irish suffragists. Many people prominent in the suffrage movement in Ireland were pacifists, notably those connected with the IWFL and the IWSF.

Up to this point women from diverse religious, social and political backgrounds had been able to unite under the common aim of votes for women. Despite disagreement over the use of militant tactics, the various Irish suffrage societies had worked together in a tenuous harmony. For English suffragists the main objective was to convince government and public alike of the equity of granting female suffrage. With contemporary developments in Irish political life, Irishwomen faced a more complex situation. Committed suffragists began to take sides on the major issues of the day, and the initial unity of the movement became increasingly strained.

(Copy)

H. M. PRISON, MOUNTJOY,

30th September, 1913.

CONVICT MARY LEIGH.

I beg to report that yesterday this woman was fed as follows:-

9 a.m. Milk, Bengers Food, and one egg...... Total 8 oz.
                                              Vomit 5 oz.

12-30 p.m. Beef juice, Brands chicken & milk. Total 8 oz.
                                               Vomit 4 oz.

5-30 p.m. Milk, Bengers Food, egg............ Total 10 oz.
                                              Vomit 3½ oz.

The stomach was washed out before the first meal.

At the 9 a.m. meal her temperature was 98.2°, her pulse 80, and her weight 75¼ lbs.

At the 5-30 p.m. meal her temperature was 96.4°, her pulse 70.

At 9 a.m. to-day her temperature was 96.6, her pulse 80, and her weight 74½ lbs, being a loss of ¾ lb. as compared with yesterday.

I find that there is a marked loss of vital power, and the case has, in my opinion, now become one of urgency.   The woman was assisted this morning while walking from her cell, and it was necessary to lift her and place her on the couch before feeding.

The pulse is weak; the urine is high coloured, acid, and contains albumen.

H. G. DOWDALL, M.D.

A medical report on Mary Leigh, during her imprisonment in Mountjoy prison.

Labour Link

In Ireland the women's cause is felt by all labour men and women as their cause...the labour cause has no more earnest and whole-hearted supporters than the militant women. [1] James Connolly

In September 1913 Constance de Markievicz declared to a meeting of the IWFL that there were three great movements going on in Ireland at that time – the national movement, the women's movement, and the industrial movement 'all fighting the same fight, for the extension of human liberty'. [2] While the influence of the nationalist movement was to prove divisive, for the women's movement that of labour held considerable promise. Reflecting on this potential Louie Bennett observed:

> A large number of the reforms we desire and hope to achieve by means of the vote are also the objective of the Labour Party. Further, the Labour Party – or rather should I say the Labour class as a whole – have realised as no other class have done, the need for the economic and political freedom of women. [3]

Acceptance of common aims and grievances paved the way for co-operation between many suffrage and labour workers, although there were exceptions on both sides.

The initial linkage between the two groups began with the broadening concern of the new suffrage organisations, culminating in the formation of the IWRL. These new groups increasingly devoted much attention to the conditions of women workers. The emergence of such women leaders as Hanna Sheehy Skeffington, Louie Bennett and Helen Chenevix was crucial for the forging of links between the labour and suffrage movements. In England, Sylvia Pankhurst was eventually forced to leave the WSPU because of her involvement with labour. She then led the East End Federation, previously a WSPU branch, as an autonomous body. The federation differed from the WSPU in some important respects; it advocated adult suffrage, it welcomed men and women, its membership was working-class and it worked closely with the labour movement. In Ireland no suffrage society could claim the same support base, but close links with the labour movement were established. The IWFL, despite its constitutional ban on political affiliation, at one time rented rooms from the Independent Labour Party of Ireland, in the Antient Concert Rooms, Great Brunswick Street in Dublin (now the Academy Theatre in Pearse Street) before moving to offices of its own in Westmoreland Street; there was some degree of dual membership.

Louie Bennett deepened the labour connection by utilising the IWRL to draw attention to the social and economic position of women workers. *Bean na hEireann* had regularly published articles advocating the organisation of women workers. Similar articles were contained in the *Irish Citizen,* whose editorials frequently pointed out the significance of the labour movement for women. Some suffrage societies became involved directly with the problems facing women at work. The IWRL conducted investigations into Dublin factories and organised public debates and seminars on the problems discovered. In 1913 the *Irish Citizen* published the findings of the IWRL work, giving examples of pay and conditions of firms in dispute with their employees. Dublin women workers were not only paid less than their male counterparts but received less than women in Belfast or England. Independently from the IWRL, the *Irish Citizen* regularly carried information on the entire spectrum of women's employment. This paper and the various women's groups constantly urged the appointment of additional women factory inspectors, as did the trade union movement. At that time there were only two such inspectors, one a woman resident in Belfast. It was pointed out that press reports of disputes often misrepresented the women workers involved. The paper urged that women workers should join trade unions and that 'women of the leisured class' should acquaint themselves with the problems of working women. Further, it was stated that 'incompetent middle-class girls who worked for little or nothing in order to earn pocket money,' supplemented by the continuous influx of country girls who would work for a pittance, were prime reasons for the depressed wages in Dublin.[4] The IWFL, acutely aware of the problem, indicated to members of the Independent Labour Party of Ireland that:

> The woman of the labouring classes today, whether as an
> industrial worker or as a wife and mother, is the most
> exploited and overdriven slave on the face of the earth....
> she has not only to win labour, but the right to labour.[5]

Indeed, not all trade unionists were over-anxious to enfranchise or unionise women of their own class, claiming fears of job loss and wage cutting. Craft unions particularly opposed the idea of admitting women. Rather than admit women and guarantee equal pay, many workers preferred to exclude women altogether. In 1910 *Bean na hEireann* reported that:

> Some leading members of the Dublin Trades Council
> have been approached regarding the organising of the
> women workers in Dublin. So far very little
> encouragement has been offered on this decidedly urgent
> question. While generally admitting the needs of the
> unorganised female worker, the male members of the
> wage earners look with suspicion of their sister slaves and
> are seemingly loath to offer any practical help.[6]

Dermot Keogh, in his research into the Dublin trade union movement, confirms these observations, noting that:

> The plight of the women workers often met with little
> sympathy from trade unionists. Generally women were
> discounted as cheap labour who could undercut trade
> union rates in a job and jeopardise the livelihoods of
> tradesmen.[7]

To solve the problem of lack of organisation among women, the call for a separate women's union was increasingly heard. The Irish Women Workers' Union (IWWU) was established on 5 September 1911 in the Antient Concert Rooms in Dublin.[8] Among those who addressed the meeting were Constance de Markievicz and Hanna Sheehy Skeffington. Delia Larkin, sister of the labour leader James (Jim) Larkin, acted as secretary to the new organisation. The Suffrage overtone was clear, as the

THE IRISH
CITIZEN

Printed in
Ireland
on
Irish Paper.

For Men and Women Equally
The Rights of Citizenship;
From Men and Women Equally
The Duties of Citizenship.

Monthly
One Penny,
Annual
Subscription
1s. 6d. post free.

Vol. 5.   DUBLIN, MARCH, 1915.   No. 36.

inaugural meeting was told 'a union such as has now been founded will not alone help you to obtain better wages, but will also be a great means of helping you get the vote.'[9]

The *Irish Citizen* maintained its active support for the labour movement throughout the 1913 lock-out, highlighting the past support trade union leaders had accorded the suffrage cause. It was pointed out that when a petition against the Cat and Mouse Act was circulated amongst members of Dublin corporation, 'no man wearing the Red Hand badge of the Transport Union refused to sign it'.[10] Suffragists from various associations gave practical help to the strikers by organising food kitchens. Some, like Hanna Sheehy Skeffington and other members of the IWFL, worked in the soup kitchen in Liberty Hall organised by Constance de Markievicz, all the time wearing their suffrage badges. Others like Louie Bennett and IWRL members participated in a scheme inititated by the Lady Mayoress, Mrs Sherlock, to aid strikers' families. The relief work greatly strengthened the bonds between labour and suffragists. Young women locked out in the dispute attended meetings of the IWFL and the *Irish Citizen* exposed the plight of the poor, again drawing attention to the need for a feminist view in Irish society:

> Larkinism and the sympathetic strike would not have
> found acceptance amongst a class who had felt that those
> in power realised their hardships and were endeavouring

to mitigate them. Only a purely masculine government could remain passive when aware of the nature of those hardships. The Dublin labour troubles are a fresh example of the need for the feminine point of view in politics.[11]

Labour journals were increasingly reflecting the influence of the new alliance. Reports of suffrage meetings and advertisements of suffrage events were supported by increasingly progressive views in the letter columns. A 'male trade unionist' writing in 1912 to the *Irish Worker,* the ITGWU newspaper edited by Jim Larkin, on the votes for women issue expressed surprise that workers could be undecided on the matter:

When the women stand for their rights we find many of the men who ought to know better, and who are themselves only permitted to vote on their masters' conditions and in their masters' interests, take pleasure in opposing their claims and in trying to cover their brave efforts with ridicule.[12]

In 1915 the *Workers' Republic,* successor to the *Irish Worker* wrote:

Several well known and experienced suffragists have kindly consented to undertake organising work in connection with the union. They are women who showed us their sympathy two years ago.[13]

The most significant figure linking the suffrage movement with organised labour was Louie Bennett. She had been born into a comfortable middle-class protestant home in Dublin. Her involvement with the suffrage movement led her to discover the conditions of working women in the city. Initially she refused to become involved in trade union work because of reservations about Connolly's policy of combining nationalist and labour activities. After 1916 she changed her position and became active in both trade union and Labour Party affairs. She was a life-long pacifist who fought against militarism in all forms. In 1916 she took over both the leadership of the IWWU and the editorship of the *Irish Citizen*. The former position was vacant through the imprisonment of Helena Molony after the rising, and the latter because of the absence in America of Hanna Sheehy Skeffington following her husband's murder by a British army officer at the time of the 1916 rising.[14] He had not been involved in the rising itself, but was arrested on his way home after attending a meeting organised to prevent looting of city centre shops. Under Louie Bennett's leadership the IWWU was reorganised on a professional basis and by January 1918 membership had reportedly risen from a few hundred to over two thousand.[15] She deliberately organised the IWWU as a separate women's union. There was much debate about the desirability of a special union for women. Defending the existence of such a union Louie Bennett argued:

> It is futile to deny a latent antagonism between the sexes
> in the world of industry. There is a disposition amongst
> men workers not only to keep women in inferior and

THOSE WHO TALK LEAST BUT SUFFER MOST IN THE DUBLIN STRIKE.

A soup kitchen in Liberty Hall shows Delia Larkin feeding some starving children.

subordinate positions, but even to drive them out of industry altogether.... Men have not the same aspirations for women as women have for themselves, and in a mixed organisation much time and trouble would have to be

Constance de Markievicz playing Joan of Arc during a pageant of famous women.

wasted in securing the co-operation of the men in a demand for reforms of which the women may feel urgent need. For it must always be bourne in mind that in mixed trade unions the men are practically always the dominant element.[16]

While she conceded the stronger bargaining power of broad-based unions, she maintained that so long as women occupied a subordinate position within the trade union movement they would need the safeguard of an independent organisation, noting that in the matter of wages: 'the increases asked for women from a trade union of men and women are less than for men; the increase accepted is nearly always considerably less than the men's.[17]

Cissie Calahan, one of the few examples of working-class involvement with the suffrage movement, defended the concept of mixed trade unions. She was active in the Linen Drapers' Assistants Association, and laid the blame for the under-involvement of women on the shoulders of the women themselves. She cited the reluctance of women to go forward as candidates for branch or executive committees that left the management of the union in male hands. She claimed that Louie Bennett was in fact advocating the perpetuation of sex antagonism, and that the division of the sexes into separate unions might prove an effective weapon for bosses at times of dispute:

> I would remind Miss Bennett that the pioneers of the suffrage movement did not seek to establish a separate parliament for women, but demanded a place in the nation's parliament. If women in the industrial world want a place in the labour movement, they must seek it in the Labour Parliament, shoulder to shoulder with the men, and not in any separate organisation apart and isolated.[18]

The debate was to continue for many years. In 1939 Helena Molony conceded that the organisation of women on sex lines was theoretically wrong but claimed that it remained a temporary necessity 'owing to the fact that women are a separate economic class'.[19] The IWWU argued:

> Women need the safeguard of an organisation
> administered and controlled by themselves on the
> grounds that their claim to equal pay for equal work is not
> recognised, that the interests of women are apt to be
> subordinated to those of men, that conditions of work are
> as important to women as rates of pay and that a women's
> union is required to deal with the incursion of badly paid
> girls into industry. Furthermore, many women maintain
> that it is impossible to ignore the question of sex and that
> many special problems arise in connection with the
> employment of women with which women themselves
> are best fitted to deal.[20]

Helena Moloney.

It was the IWWU in 1935 which, through strike action by laundry workers, first won the right to paid annual holidays for workers.

In addition to her union work Louie Bennett maintained her connections with the IWRL and stressed the need for organisation if the vote was to be of any real value. Through the pages of the *Irish Citizen* she expressed views similar to those of James Connolly:

> The rapid development of organisation in the Irishwomen's world of labour is the best possible contribution to the whole cause of feminism. There can be no real freedom and independence for women until they are economically free. [21]

Under the aegis of the IWWU, the Irish Nurses Union (INU) was established, one of the first of its kind in Europe. The horror of the *Irish Times'* appeal to nurses showed the depth of opposition to women's organisation that still existed. Nurses were asked:

> ...not to unthrone and degrade the profession by dallying with the promises of Trade Unionism. A strike of nurses would be hardly less painful and disconcerting than a strike of wives in favour, of say, a forty-hour week of domestic activity. [22]

By 1920 the *Irish Citizen* was devoting a special page to women workers 'in accordance with the policy of feminism, peace and labour', for which it had always stood. [23] The page detailed the activities of the women's unions, pay claims and branch affairs. Eventually the IWWU and the INU decided to use the *Irish Citizen* as their official journal and source of communication with members throughout the country. The interaction of the suffrage and labour movements was thus producing new bonds and inevitably new demands for radical approaches on the women's question. The IWWU appealed to readers of the *Irish Citizen* to influence women workers to join the union. Trade unionists and socialists such as William

O'Brien, Walter Carpenter, Nora Connolly, Tom Johnson and Cathal O'Shannon were among those who addressed meetings of the IWFL, the latter seeking the co-operation of militant suffragettes in organising women workers. An *Irish Citizen* editorial reflected upon the changes that had taken place and the increasing role that women had played:

> Persons in pigtails are displaying qualities which a few short years ago were deemed exceptional even among the leaders of the women's movement. As the women organise, new leaders, many far away from voting age, spring up to guide them.... It is good to remember that Irish Suffragists have always advocated Trade Unionism, and that in the great revival which followed Easter 1916, prominent Irish Suffragists played a leading part. [24]

How did the political arm of the labour movement view feminist ideals and co-operation with the suffrage movement? In 1909 Jim Larkin, disparagingly described by the *Westminister Gazette* as a 'kind of labour suffragette', placed adult suffrage at the head of the immediate measures to be advocated by an Irish Labour Party. At The Independent Labour Party of Ireland's inaugural meeting in Belfast on 17 May 1912, and again at its first Dublin meeting the following month, a resolution demanding the inclusion of votes for women in the Home Rule bill was passed. The *Irish Citizen* noted approvingly the aims of the new party for complete political and social equality between the sexes. While adult suffrage was the ultimate aim, the paper reported that all speakers at the meetings recognised the logic of demanding that the local government register should be embodied in the Home Rule bill. [25] There were, however, some mixed feeling in the ranks of labour, not just about votes for women, but women's rights in general. At the 1912 Irish Trades Union Congress a motion demanding advert suffrage proposed by Larkin and seconded by William O'Brien, exposed the divisions that were still beneath the surface. Mr Nolan, from Dublin, representing the National Union of Book-binders agreed that women's status as wage earners should be raised but feared that granting the vote would 'tend to take away from the peace of the home', resulting in 'the destruction of that nobility of character for which their women are prized'.[26] The major source of division between suffrage campaigners and labour representatives was not however on the basic conviction, but as Hanna Sheehy Skeffington noted, more essential class lines, 'organised labour wanted women to help them press for adult suffrage, ridiculing women's suffrage as 'votes for ladies'.[27] There was some justification to this accusation. The existing franchise was property based, and if extended would obviously only benefit middle-class women. There were those who feared that what Hanna Sheehy Skeffington described as 'votes for ladies' would increase the representation of the capitalist class through the enfranchisement of what was traditionally regarded as a conservative and clerically influenced section of that class. At the 1914 Irish Trades Union Congress Larkin made the point that suffrage could be used for or against the working class. Connolly however stated that he was in favour of giving women the vote 'even if they used it against him as a human right'.[28] In seeking the parliamentary vote for women who already possessed the local government vote, which was also property based, the IWSLGA would have argued that any section of women possessing the vote would improve living and working conditions of women in general. Such views could be interpreted as an extension of the same paternalistic attitudes which suffrage societies accused enfranchised males of possessing, i.e. – women did not need the vote because they were already represented by their menfold. Marie Johnson, who had worked in the offices of the Irish Textile Workers Union in Belfast, and whose husband Tom Johnson was later the leader of the Irish Labour Party, writing about her introduction to the suffrage movement, indicates how aware working-class women were of the limitations of some of the suffrage movement's positions:

> The first demand was for the vote for women of property distinctly, i.e. a certain class who considered themselves as important to the country, and to share in legislation as the men who had the vote. We ordinaries resented this, but did not refuse to support, as we were assured that our turn would come.[29]

Consistently in the pages of the *Irish Citizen* and at meetings of the IWFL and the IWRL, the economic position of women was equated with their voteless condition. Commenting on a letter from Winifred Carney, secretary of the Irish Textile Workers Union in Belfast, regarding the conditions of Belfast linen workers the paper stated:

> Without political power to enforce their economic necessities, the sweated women workers of Belfast are virtually powerless to secure the legislative changes which they demand. [30]

James Connolly continued this theme when he told the IWFL:

> It was because women workers had no vote that they had not the safeguards even of the laws passed for their protection because these were ignored. They had women working for wages on which a man could not keep a dog. Men's conditions bad as they were, had been improved because of the vote. [31]

Winifred Carney.

Connolly, described by the *Irish Citizen* as the 'soundest and most thorough going feminist among all the Irish labour men' was a frequent speaker at suffrage meetings. Hanna Sheehy Skeffington noted in her memoirs that Connolly never failed to respond to a call for a meeting or a protest demonstration. He held meetings for the IWFL in Belfast, and travelled to speak on the embattled IWFL platform in Dublin during the troubled days after the Asquith visit. Speaking to an unanimously adopted motion at the 1913 Irish Trades Union Congress condemning government restrictions on suffrage meetings, Connolly stated that until women were made equal politically they could only be half free.[32] During the 1913 lock-out class tensions became more acute. Walter Carpenter of the Independent Labour Party was among those who addressed IWFL meetings and urged men to throw in their lot with the league and never mind its militance. Eva Gore Booth, sister of Constance de Markievicz, travelled from Manchester where she was active in the organisation of women mill workers, and highlighted the fact that women's grievances were inextricably linked to their voteless condition. The IWFL's London branch held collections for the Dublin strikers and in November 1913, the *Daily Herald*, a London socialist newspaper, held a hugh meeting at the Albert Hall in London to generate solidarity for Dublin and to demand the release of the then imprisoned Larkin. Militant Suffragette followers of Charlotte Despard and Sylvia Pankhurst were heavily involved in organising the meeting. Connolly was loudly cheered when he declared that he stood for opposition to the domination of nation over nation, class over class and sex over sex. Sylvia Pankhurst's appearance on the platform precipitated her expulsion from the WSPU.[33] Christabel had severed all links with labour claiming that the great need for the time was for women to learn to stand and act alone. Henry Harben, a supporter of the Daily Herald League (a socialist group with a branch in Dublin) and a one time adviser to Christabel, wrote to her after the Albert Hall meeting, claiming that most of the speakers:

> were obviously giving the women lip-service and
> dragging them in as an afterthought. There was no real

feeling on the woman question. The ovation to Sylvia was
to the rebel and not to the woman.[34]

In this context it is interesting to note Connolly's address to
the IWFL later that month. He claimed to have championed the
women's cause not merely because they were women, but
because they were in rebellion. Suffragettes, according to
Connolly, could only succeed by subordinating everything,
regardless of the consequences, to the attainment of their
objective. Later, addressing suffragists in Belfast, he broadened
his view of tactics, stressing that propaganda for the vote should
be accompanied by the more immediate prospect of better
conditions and pay. These policies were similar to those of
Sylvia Pankhurst's East End Federation. The *Irish Worker*
reported on a series of meetings held to discuss Connolly's
suggestions, that 'labour ideas and ideals are entering in, and
these three meetings will make excellent propaganda.'[35] But
propaganda for whom? Many Belfast suffragists expressed the
fear that to follow Connolly's advice would side-track the
suffrage movement. Henry Harben voiced similar fears in
correspondence with Christabel Pankhurst after the Albert Hall
meeting in what many today might consider a remarkably
prophetic way:

> I feel that our statesmanship should be to make the fullest
> use for the women of the enthusiasms of the moment
> without risking the betrayals of the future. If for fear of
> these latter, you women stand aloof too much, you will
> lose something which might be of priceless value in the
> next two years. If, on the other hand, for the sake of these
> apparent temporary advantages, you associate yourselves
> in any way with us, you will fray off in the future, and
> your women will become what the women of the
> previous movements became; merely the handmaidens of
> a man's movement.[36]

The question of women's co-operation and involvement with
other movements was a vexed one in Ireland as elsewhere. The
IWFL was closest to formal alliance with labour through the

beliefs of individual members if not official League policy. Frank Sheehy Skeffington actually urged temporary alliance. In a letter to a Belfast suffrage leader in March 1914 he wrote:

> The militants are now more popular in Dublin, far more popular with the masses than John Redmond, because they drew close to Labour in the recent troubles.... Ultimately your strength in Belfast will come from an alliance – open or tacit – with militant labour... Sylvia Pankhurst's policy is, I am satisfied, the right one for industrial centres. [37]

The IWRL also favoured close collaboration with the Labour Party. In 1914 however, when Louie Bennett was incorrectly quoted as advocating union with that party, she hastened to point out:

> I do not think it would ever be advisable to form a union with any party. Suffragists must continue to take their own stand independent of any political party. I am with those suffragists who believe they will find firm allies amongst the Labour people. But that is not to advocate a union with the Labour Party...suffragists and labourites might do mutual services for each other whilst remaining absolutely independent. [38]

Inevitably some opposition to a labour alliance rested solely on class lines. One Belfast suffragist disdained:

> The Labour movement was very young and its ranks were taken from the lowest. It was not the gentlemen and gentlewomen who sneered at them, but it was the scum, and it would be very dangerous to seek alliance with that party. [39]

Support for co-operation with labour was stronger in Dublin than elsewhere. The greater diversity of suffrage groups and the bonds struck during 1913 account for this. Close identification with the labour movement did not inhibit criticism were it felt necessary. At the time of the Irish

Mrs Charlotte Despard.

Convention in 1917, the *Irish Citizen* reported:

> When Labour Sunday was celebrated in Dublin a few
> weeks ago, no woman was invited to stand on the
> platform by the Labour Party. The women of Ireland
> might all have been free to enjoy the comforts of a home,
> a fireside, and a cradle to rock for all the interest the
> Labour Party of Ireland manifested in their affairs. [40]

Again in 1918, Louie Bennett recorded the great
disappointment felt by the IWWU that no reference was made
at the All-Ireland Labour Conference to the women's part in the
campaign against conscription. Commenting on the local
elections of 1920 the *Irish Citizen* dryly remarked 'official labour
has the unenviable distinction of entirely ignoring women on
their ticket.'[41] Was this evidence that the labour movement was
already about to jettison women and that the alliance was
suitable only in so far as it benefitted the cause of labour?

Up to the early twentieth century there had been little contact
between the labour and suffrage movements. The involvement
of young socialist oriented feminists in the suffrage campaign
from 1908 onwards coincided with a recognition by some
labour leaders of common disabilities shared by men and
women. As the women's movement organised and radicalised,
labour leaders saw its potential as an ally. Hanna Sheehy
Skeffington claimed that Connolly recognised from the first the
latent possibilities, and a number of feminists also saw the
possible advantages of alliance. Crises strengthened the bonds.
The 1913 dispute greatly accelerated activity and a sense of
common purpose combined with an understanding of separate
aims ensued. Despite frequent allusions to the advantages of
co-operation, organisations such as the IWFL and the IWRL
deliberately remained non-party. In 1920 the *Irish Citizen*
perhaps explained the philosophy behind this clinging to
independence when it stated that 'no party, unhappily, is yet
quite free from sin where women are concerned.'[42]

The primary influence of both groups can be found in the
wording of the 1916 Proclamation which was addressed to both
Irish men and women and guaranteed equal rights and equal

opportunities to all citizens. Hanna Sheehy Skeffington
credited this provision to Connolly, but he replied that only
one had questioned it.[43] The other main area of influence
between the two movements can be gauged by the traffic from
the suffrage movement into the ranks of labour. Connolly had
advised suffragists to involve themselves in the organisation of
working women, not simply for the suffrage but also for their
material benefit. Hanna Sheehy Skeffington notes in her
memoirs that through the suffrage cause many hitherto
protected and comfortable women were made aware of those
less fortunate and became social rebels. Louie Bennett, Helen
Chenevix, and Helena Molony were to commit their lives to the
IWWU. By contrast the involvement of working-class women in
the suffrage movement was minimal. In 1930 Helena Molony
wrote:

> The Women's movement, now unhappily long spent,
> which aroused such a deep feeling of social consciousness
> and revolt among women of a more favoured class,
> passed over the heads of the Irish working woman and
> left her untouched. [44]

The strong agricultural base of Irish society militated against
a cohesive national suffrage movement, and by the time women
workers were becoming effectively organised industrially in a
position to join forces with the suffrage campaign, the first
installment of women's suffrage was already in sight. The
national question then dominated to preclude the development
of a strong united post-suffrage women's movement.

Constance de Markievicz speaking to the IWFL in 1915 had
exhorted women to:

> Take up your responsibilities and be prepared to go your
> own way depending for safety on your own courage, your
> own truth, and your own common sense, and not on the
> problematic chivalry of the the men you may meet on the
> way. The two brilliant classes of women who follow this
> higher ideal are Suffragettes and the Trades Union or
> Labour women. In them lies the hope of the future. But for

Emmeline and Sylvia Pankhurst in Holloway prison.

them women are everywhere today in a position of inferiority. [45]

Similarly a prominent member of the IWFL stated in 1918:

> I have no difficulty in imagining a time when the two
> great world problems of woman and labour shall fuse into
> one, for they have a great and natural affinity. Political
> ferment in this country has... almost eclipsed every other
> movement in the popular mind ...when the shouting and
> the tumult has died down the two world forces of
> feminism and labour will again emerge and dominate the
> situation.[46]

Labour undoubtedly played a significant role in the women's
cause in Ireland, and the continuing advance of women in the
period immediately after the 1914-18 war may be said to owe
much to the alliance of labour and feminists. Other influences
were not to be so beneficial, however.

An advertisement of the day.

Splinters of War

Votes for Women Now – Damn Your War. [1]

From 1914 the cohesiveness of the suffrage movement in Ireland was threatened by two developments – the outbreak of war, and the burgeoning separatist movement. Indeed the women's suffrage campaign internationally became one of the many casualities of the war which started in August 1914. The situation varied from country to country, but everywhere the movement was dealt a severe blow and international co-operation between women became almost impossible. Some sections of the women's movement attempted to transcend the situation. A manifesto headed 'Stop the War' was issued by the International Suffrage Alliance, pointing out that the fate of Europe depended on decisions which women had no power to shape. In England all suffrage militancy was suspended and most societies there became totally involved in relief work of various kinds. The WSPU not only ceased militancy, but closed its offices, dismissed its organisers and became involved in various forms of war work and propaganda, including the active encouragement of recruiting men for the army. [2] There was much dissatisfaction among members at the action of the WSPU leaders. Ultimately the organisation disintegrated. From 1915 its weekly paper *The Suffragette* was rechristened *Britannia* and was devoted to anti-German propaganda.

Suffrage societies in Ireland varied in their response to the war. Some abandoned or postponed all suffrage work and became involved in 'war-relief' works. These tended to be those societies most closely associated with English groups, and were the ones most offended by the anti-war stance of the *Irish Citizen*. The letters column of the paper displayed the breach between suffrage groups as those who justified involvement in 'war work' were condemned by those who viewed such activities as a negation of true suffrage policy. Editorials constantly reiterated the opposition of the *Irish Citizen* to such relief works on the part of suffrage societies as being inconsistent with the principle of suffrage first. The degree to which Irish suffrage societies became involved in such work varied. The IWSLGA included amongst its list of works the

STOP THE WAR !

MANIFESTO BY THE INTERNATIONAL
SUFFRAGE ALLIANCE.

We, the women of the world, view
with apprehension and dismay the
present situation in Europe, which
threatens to involve one continent, if
not the whole world, in the disasters
and horrors of war. In this terrible
hour, when the fate of Europe depends
on decisions which women have no
power to shape, we, realising our re-
sponsibilies as the mothers of the
race, cannot stand passive by. Powerless though we are politically, we call
upon the Governments and Powers of
our several countries to avert the
threatened unparalleled disaster. In
none of the countries immediately concerned in the threatened outbreak have
women any direct power to control the
political destinies of their own countries. They find themselves on the
brink of the almost unbearable position of seeing all that they most reverence and treasure, the home, the
family, the race, subjected not merely
to risks, but to certain and extensive
damage which they are powerless
either to avert or to assuage. Whatever its result the conflict will leave
mankind the poorer, will set back
civilisation, and will be a powerful
check to the gradual amelioration in
the condition of the masses of the
people, on which so much of the real
welfare of nations depend.

We women of twenty-six countries,
having banded ourselves together in
the International Women's Suffrage
Alliance with the object of obtaining
our political means of sharing with
men the power which shapes the fate
of nations, appeal to you to leave
untried no method of conciliation or
arbitration for arranging international
differences which may help to avert
deluging half the civilised world in
blood.

Printed in *The Irish
Citizen,* just prior to the
outbreak of the 1st
World War.

establishment of an emergency fund for the relief of Belgian refugees in Ireland, women's patrols in Dublin and Belfast, an Irish advisory committee for the prevention and relief of distress caused by war, and the endowment of a bed in the Dublin Castle Red Cross Hospital, awkwardly titled 'The Irish Women's Suffrage and Local Government Association Bed'.[3] Their branches throughout the country were similiarly engaged in relief works. In an attempt to involve women in some form of war-relief work without abandoning their suffrage objectives, an emergency council of Irish Suffragists was formed. This council hoped 'to fulfill the demands the present situation makes on all civilians', without entirely suspending propaganda work. In a letter to the *Freeman's Journal* the council stated:

> While recognising the imperative necessity for organised remedial work, and while taking part therein, we wish to emphasis our conviction that the claim for the enfranchisement of women must not be blotted out, even at the present crisis. All the conditions which are the outcome of the present situation prove more than ever the absolute necessity for the enfranchisement of women.[4]

Among the societies supporting the emergency council was the IWSF, and relief work was carried on in workrooms in Dublin where about a hundred young women were employed.[5] Initially on the outbreak of war, the federation decided to suspend active suffrage propaganda and to concentrate on relief work. This policy was changed in 1915 when the executive declared that the object of the IWSF was the enfranchisement of Irish women, and that all philanthropic activities must be regarded as of secondary importance. Members were therefore urged to work for attainment of this objective before the end of the war. In Cork the MWFL bought an ambulance and presented it to the military authorities. This action forced Mary MacSwiney, by now a committed republican, to sever her connections with the suffrage movement, as she had come to the conclusion that the majority of the league were 'Britons first, suffragists second, and

Irishwomen perhaps a bad third'.[6] The IWFL remained firmly opposed to such activities. It pointed out that during the labour dispute in Dublin the previous year widespread distress and suffering had occurred, without any such concerted action on the part of women. Individuals amongst suffragists had been free then, as now, to give what aid they could, but it was recognised clearly that relief works were outside the scope of their organisations:

> Our movement was founded with the definite aim of securing the political freedom of women. To this work, we have pledged ourselves and to no other... The European war has done nothing to alter our condition of slavery. It has only served to make us realise more deeply the utter helplessness and defencelessness of our position as political outcasts.[7]

In a letter to Hanna Sheehy Skeffington in October 1914, Louie Bennett expressed her dissatisfaction with the position of women's organisation which were, with the exception of the IWFL, '...like sheep astray, and I suppose when the necessity of knitting socks is over – the order will be – Bear Sons. And those of us who can't will feel we had better get out of the way as quickly as we can.'[8]

Over and above disagreement on the propriety of suffrage societies becoming involved in war-relief works loomed the larger quesion of war and militarism as opposed to feminism and pacifism. Christabel Pankhurst had stated that 'as suffragettes we could not be pacifists at any price'.[9] Not all suffragettes agreed with her and many, including her sisters, Sylvia and Adela, became involved in pacifist organisations. Likewise, many Irish suffragists were convinced pacifists, and the *Irish Citizen* adopted a strong anti-militarist stance, which was reflected in its leading articles and letters pages. Frank Sheehy Skeffington in an article on war and feminism put forward the view that, 'War is necessarily bound up with the destruction of feminism.... Feminism is necessarily bound up with the abolition of war.... If we want to stop war we must begin by stopping this war'.[10] Another article by a member of the IWFL stated that:

> We are opposed to this war, as we are opposed to all war,
> because we are profoundly convinced that war is in itself
> an unmitigated evil and the greatest existing menace to
> true human progress.... It is our conviction feminism and
> militarism are natural born enemies and cannot flourish
> on the same soil.[11]

Such sentiments were being echoed in feminist organisations
throughout the world, and Ireland was not the only country in
which suffragists were divided on the issue. An Irish branch of
the Women's International League for Peace and Freedom was
established, and carried on peace propaganda during the war
years. A women's International Peace Congress was organised
for the Hague in April 1915. Of the seven Irish women
delegates only Louie Bennett was granted a travel permit, while
in England only twenty four out of 180 delegates were granted
permits. As events transpired only one or two Englishwomen
reached the Hague as the British Admiralty banned all
passenger traffic on the day most of the women were to travel.
A public protest meeting was organised in Dublin by the IWFL
against the government action. At this meeting James Connolly
and Thomas MacDonagh, both to be signatories of the 1916
proclamation, spoke.

From this point on, the conflicting ideals of war and
militarism versus feminism and pacifism were viewed not
solely in the broad European context, but increasingly in the
developing militaristic atmosphere in Ireland. When Padraic
Pearse sent a letter of support to the Dublin protest meeting he
concluded by saying that 'the present incident will do good if it
ranges more of the women definitely with the national
forces'.[12] The chairwoman of the meeting asked in reply why it
should not range more of the national forces definitely with the
women? Thomas MacDonagh in speaking to the meeting
agreed with the chairwoman in her remarks, and promised he
would lose no opportunity of pressing for women's rights.
However, while he agreed with the women in their pacifist
principles he acted as apologist for the rising spirit of militarism

in Ireland. He admitted that his position as an advocate of peace was an anomalous one, as he was one of the founders and organisers of the Irish Volunteers. His one apology for his part in the creation of a different kind of militarism in Ireland was that they were not going to exploit their own people, and he hoped and knew that it would never be used against their fellow countrymen.[13]

Louie Bennett, commenting on the meeting, wrote that 'militarism, in the most subtly dangerous form, has its hold upon Ireland'.[14] MacDonagh's speech brought a response from Frank Sheehy Skeffington in the form of an open letter to Thomas MacDonagh. In this Skeffington enunciated clearly the views of pacifist feminism towards militarism and in particular towards Irish militarism. He pointed out that most militarist systems had started with the same high ideals as the Irish Volunteers professed. His suggestion that the executive of the Volunteers state definitely that it stood for the liberties of Irish People without distinction of sex, class or creed, had been refused. Pointing to the omission of women from the three fundamental objects of the association, Skeffington stated:

> It is in the highest degree significant that women are left out. Why are they left out? Consider carefully why; and when you have found and clearly expressed the reason why women cannot be asked to enroll in the movement, you will be close to the reactionary element in the movement itself.[15]

So we find that the small group of peace advocates were to become increasingly unpopular both with belligerent imperialists and militant nationalists. On the purely anti-war front various groups could unite. One example of this was the strenuous opposition which developed against attempts to introduce conscription into Ireland.

Feminist and socialist organisations disintegrated worldwide under the impact of war. It was not the war that produced the most damaging effects on the women's movement in Ireland, however, but rather the developing and accelerating course of Irish politics. During the 1912-14 period, the Irish women's suffrage movement had had to withstand a number of divisive developments, mainly connected with the Home Rule agitation. The war again caused division in the ranks. Unlike England, however, most Irish suffrage societies remained in existence during and after the war. In fact, one new society was launched during the war years.[16] The Irish Catholic Women's Suffrage Association was formed in Dublin in 1915, and the IWFL established a branch in Belfast after the WSPU closed its office there.[17] An Irish branch of the Protestant English Church League for Women's Suffrage had been in existence since 1913. Increasingly, however, the energies of many suffragists were drawn into the political struggles of the time. From 1914 onwards, with Home Rule on the statute book, it was the growing separatist movement which created the greatest obstacle to a united women's movement.

VOTES FOR WOMEN

Why not have a **COSY TEA**

in the

Suffrage Tea Room

WESTMORELAND CHAMBERS,

WESTMORELAND STREET

(Opposite Bewley's)

•

Popular Prices

Home-made Cakes, etc.

Free Meetings held every Tuesday in the Antient Concert Buildings, 8 o'c.; Open Discussion. All Welcome

Irish Women's Franchise League

CORRIGAN & WILSON, Arville Place, Dublin.

Pamphlet advertising Irish Women's Franchise League meetings.

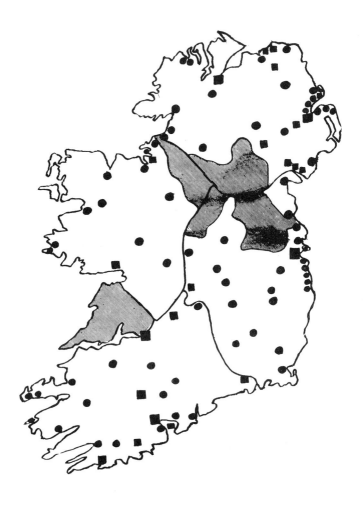

Suffrage Map depicting the number of suffrage societies throughout Ireland, *The Irish Citizen*.

Suffrage First Before All Else

I would ask every Nationalist woman to pause before she joined a Suffrage Society or Franchise League that did not include in their Programme the Freedom of their Nation. A Free Ireland with No Sex Disabilities in her Constitution should be the motto of all Nationalist women.[1] Constance de Markievicz

By 1913 there were eighteen suffrage societies with a further eleven branches in Ireland catering for women of varying political, social and religious backgrounds. Yet, as a writer to the *Irish Citizen* pointed out, there was no nationalist women's franchise association 'wherein nationalists would have the opportunity to serve the cause of their sex without compromising their nationalism'.[2] A common criticism of Irish suffrage societies was that they were merely branches of English societies. Such criticisms had been one of the reasons for the formation of the IWFL, which, although agreeing to co-operate where possible with suffrage societies of other countries, had as one of the main reasons for its formation 'the different political situation of Ireland, as between a subject country seeking freedom from England, and England, a free country'.[3] Indeed, much criticism was directed not against the principle of women's suffrage, but against the propriety of Irish women seeking the vote from an alien government. The policy of the *Irish Citizen* in demanding 'suffrage first – before all else' led to conflict with those who chose to put other issues first, be it Home Rule or war work. Agnes O'Farrelly, a member of the Gaelic League and later in life a professor of the National University, articulated this disagreement from the nationalist side:

> Are we or are we not fighting for the vote before all other things? Some of us certainly are not. Keenly anxious as we are for the ordinary rights of citizenship for ourselves, we give woman suffrage second place to a charter of freedom – or some measure of freedom – for at all events, the men of our own country![4]

That some nationalist women were concerned about the status of women is evident from the pages of *Bean na hEireann* where the views of nationalist women on the suffrage issue are first encountered. In 1909 its editorial stated:

> We do not refuse to join the women's franchise movement... but we decline to join with Parliamentarians and Unionists in trying to force a Bill through Westminster.... Freedom for our Nation and the complete removal of all disabilities to our sex will be our battlecry. [5]

Some nationalist women, however, were keen suffragists, and for a time it was possible for them to maintain allegiance to both causes. Such women included Mary Colum, Mary MacSwiney, Rosamund Jacob, a member of Sinn Fein from Waterford, Constance de Markievicz and Jennie Wyse Power. Constance de Markievicz, described by Hanna Sheehy Skeffington as 'not a feminist ever and only a mild suffragist' had been an early supporter of women's suffrage. [6] In 1896 she had presided over the first suffrage meeting held in her homeplace, Drumcliffe, County Sligo, and had helped to form a branch there of the IWSLGA. [7] From about 1907 she ceased to be actively involved in the movement. Despite her disagreement with the IWFL on their policies and aims, she attended many of their public meetings and helped the League in fund-raising and publicity ventures. She equated Ireland's position as a subject nation with the position of Irish women, laying the blame for both with England:

> As our country has had her Freedom and her Nationhood taken from her by England, so also our sex is denied emancipation and citizenship by the same enemy. So therefore the first step on the road to freedom is to realize ourselves as Irishwomen – not as Irish or merely as women, but as Irishwomen doubly enslaved and with a double battle to fight. [8]

Implicit in her argument was the view that once independence was attained, the goal of 'A Free Ireland with no

Rosamund Jacob.

Sex Disabilities in her Constitution' would be achieved.

From 1912 onwards it became increasingly difficult for some women to combine membership of a suffrage society with their political beliefs. Comparison can be made with the anti-slavery campaign in the United States where women workers in that movement met with hostility from male abolitionists who claimed that it would damage the cause to connect it with the campaign for women's rights. It was argued that 'to agitate the women's amendment would defeat negro suffrage.'[9] During the crucial Home Rule years of 1912-14 this type of argument was consistently made towards suffragists by male and female Home Rulers. Fears of endangering the Home Rule bill caused many Irishwomen to submerge their suffrage views.

As soon as Home Rule appeared assured, pressure was applied towards obtaining an amendment to the bill which would enfranchise Irish women on the basis of the local government register. Elizabeth Bloxham in a letter to the *Irish Independent* identified herself as '...one of the very many nationalist women who have refrained from taking any step in connection with the suffrage movement ...that might in any way jeopardise the passing of the Home Rule Bill.'[10] She now appealed to John Redmond to ensure that Home Rule would mean freedom for women as well as men. Mary Hayden also entered the debate stating in the *Freeman's Journal* that:

> Numbers of nationalists have abstained from raising the question merely from fear that they might embarrass the government and delay the passage of the Home Rule bill. Now this danger no longer exists; an easy way lies open for removing the grievances at one stroke.[11]

Efforts were made to heal the breach between suffragists and nationalists, and to present a united demand for a women's suffrage amendment. In reply to such an appeal by Hanna Sheehy Skeffington, Jennie Wyse Power wrote:

> Nationalist women refrained from placing their suffrage views before the Irish Parliamentary Party while that Party was carrying the Home Rule bill through the English House of Commons. Now, however, the situation has quite changed, and those of us who are Irish Nationalists can only hope that an appeal at this time for the extension of the suffrage to Irishwomen will not fall on unheeding ears.... This is a time when all Irishwomen should come together, and put their views forward from an Irish standpoint in the hope that they may be allowed to exercise their right to participate in the government of their own country.[12]

A deputation of militant and non-militant suffragists travelled to London to petition for such an amendment but neither Redmond nor Asquith would receive them. In March 1914 the Sinn Fein party organised a conference in Dublin to consider the proposed exclusion of Ulster from the impending Home Rule settlement. Jennie Wyse Power, Constance de Markievicz and Hanna Sheehy Skeffington urged that Ulster women must

Mary Hayden.

not be excluded without their views being consulted in a referendum. This notion was ruled out of order by the chairman, Arthur Griffith. The following month a larger and more representative conference was held, at which Griffith put forward an alternative scheme to exclusion, including many changes in the franchise. The alteration of the franchise so as to include women was moved and received a great deal of support, but was squashed by Griffith's opposition to it as a 'social question'.[13]

From 1914, with Home Rule on the statute book, it was the growing separatist movement which posed the greatest threat to a united women's movement. The secretary of the Belfast branch of the IWFL in a report to Hanna Sheehy Skeffington stated that 'I had the Connolly girls here last night. They will join but cannot undertake to do any work as they are connected with some Irish association in which they would get into trouble if they took a prominent part in Suffrage work'.[14] While the *Irish Citizen* editorial argued 'there can be no free nation without free women', the counter-argument was made that 'neither can there be free women in an enslaved nation'.[15] With this polarisation of opinion a widening breach developed between feminists and nationalists. The formation of Cumann na mBan in April 1914 crystallised the differences between those who sought freedom first and equal rights second, and those who sought 'suffrage first – before all else'. Laurence Kettle, general secretary of the Irish Volunteers, had stated in Dublin at the formation of that group in November 1913 that there would also be work for women to do in the organisation. Lil Conlon, active in Cumann na mBan in Cork, noted that this acted as a clarion call to the women of Ireland 'the response being spontaneous, their co-operation had been solicited.'[16] What would this work be? When the question of female participation in the Volunteers had first been raised in 1913, Padraic Pearse had written to Chrissie Doyle, a former member of Inghinidhe na hEireann:

> We have been so busy grappling with the immediate problem of organising and drilling the men... that we have not yet had time to consider in any detail the work of the

women. First of all there will be ambulance and Red Cross work for them, and then I think a women's rifle club is desirable. I would not like the idea of women drilling and marching in the ordinary way but there is no reason why they should not learn to shoot.[17]

An article in the *Irish Volunteer* suggested that Irishwomen should do their duty in the Volunteer movement by forming ambulance corps, learning first aid, making flags and doing any necessary embroidery work on badges and uniforms, the writer asking 'To a patriotic Irishwoman could there be any work of more intense delight than this.'[18] All of which seemed remarkably similar to the 'war-work' engaged in by other groups of Irishwomen, and for which they had been severely criticised. The organisation of women supporters of the Volunteers got underway, and in April 1914 the first public meeting of the Irishwomen's Council, thereafter known as Cumann na mBan, was held at Wynns Hotel in Dublin. This inaugural meeting was presided over by Agnes O'Farrelly, and a provisional executive was elected. The constitution stated:

Cumann na mBan is an independent body of Irish women pledged to work for the establishment of an Irish Republic, by organising and training the women of Ireland to take their places by the side of those who are working and fighting for a free Ireland.[19]

The first task they set themselves – to initiate a Defence of Ireland fund for arming and equipping the Volunteers – brought much criticism from suffragists. This was articulated in the *Irish Citizen* editorial which deplored the:

Slavish attitude of a group of women who have just formed an 'Irishwomen's Council', not to take any forward action themselves, but to help the men of the Irish Volunteers to raise money for their equipment, in general toady to them as the Ulster Unionist Women have done to the Ulster Volunteers.

The editorial went on to state that 'Such women deserve nothing but contempt, and will assuredly earn it, not only from the freeminded members of their own sex but also from the very men to whom they "do homage" to quote the cringing words of Miss O'Farrelly.' [20]

Such strong criticism engendered counter-criticism. Mary MacSwiney, who had left the suffrage movement in Cork because of the MWFL's involvement in war-work, wrote to the *Irish Citizen* fully supporting the action of Cumann na mBan and accused that paper of alienating nationalists from the suffrage cause. Further public disagreement on the issue was expressed through the pages of the paper, some reiterating Mary MacSwiney's view that the attitude of the *Irish Citizen* would harm the suffrage cause. [21] The controversy was continued in the pages of the national press. Hanna Sheehy Skeffington attended a meeting of Cumann na mBan, and later accused the society of being merely 'an animated collecting box,' stating that:

> The proposed 'Ladies Auxiliary Committee' has
> apparently no function beyond that of a conduit pipe to
> pour a stream of gold into the coffers of the male
> organisation, and to be turned off automatically as soon as
> it had served this mean and subordinate purpose. [22]

A report of the same meeting by the *Irish Volunteer* notes that many of Hanna Sheehy Skeffington's remarks on the women's suffrage movement did not meet with the approval of the majority of the meeting. [23] Her criticisms were challenged by a number of correspondents in the national press. One of these stated:

> There is a large class of Irishwomen (and they claim to be
> self-respecting Irishwomen) who believe that they are
> represented at the polls and on the battlefields by their
> husbands, fathers, or sons who want neither vote, nor
> rifle, nor stone to help them in asserting their rights, who
> are willing to act as conduit pipes or collecting boxes or
> armour polishers, or do any other good thing that would
> help on the cause. [24]

The two honorary secretaries of Cumann na mBan – Mary Colum, and Louise Gavan Duffy, both keen Irish language enthusiasts who had taught at Pearse's school for girls in Rathmines, published a letter outlining the aims of the association:

> We are a nationalist women's political organisation and we propose to engage in any patriotic work that comes within the scope of our objects and constitution. We consider at the moment that helping to equip the Irish Volunteers is the most necessary national work. We may mention that many of the members of our Society are keen suffragists, but as an organisation we must confine ourselves within the four walls of our constitution. [25]

When in June 1914 the Irish Volunteers were in effect 'taken over' by John Redmond, the non-party stance of that organisation, and inevitably of Cumann na mBan, was cast in doubt. The *Irish Citizen* editorial was not slow to point out that fact, and to ask if the suffragists within Cumann na mBan were prepared to support a movement now controlled by 'the leading anti-suffragist politician in Ireland.' The same editorial

Mary McSwiney.

also pointed out that Redmond had already undermined the work of Cumann na mBan by establishing a new body – The Irish Volunteer Aid Association – to do precisely the same auxiliary work which Cumann na mBan had undertaken. This new association was officered and governed by men. Women could join, subscribe and work for it, but no woman had a place on its committee.[26] While some dissident voices were raised at the acquiescence of Cumann na mBan, most branches continued with their established fund-raising and other duties. In the aftermath of the 1916 rising, with large-scale imprisonment of male republicans, Cumann na mBan was destined to play a more active role. However, as late as 1919 the IWFL was still critical of the organisation:

> The women are emphatically not a force in the popular
> movement – they have no status and no influence in its
> local councils, they just cling on pathetically to the skirts
> of the movement, and are looked upon rather in the light
> of an ornamental trimming – useful to give a picturesque
> touch on occasion and, of course, to carry on the
> traditional role of auxiliaries which so many generations
> of slave women have been content to accept as their
> meed.[27]

The basic disagreement between Irish nationalist women and Irish suffragists would appear to have been one of priorities, as described in a letter to the *Irish Citizen* in 1914:

> If there is ignorance of the suffrage to be overcome in
> Ireland, it is that type of ignorance which has its roots in a
> false conception of freedom and nationhood, and which is
> unable to grasp the simple fact that the freedom of Irish
> Womanhood is a vital and indispensable factor in true
> Irish Nationhood, not a mere trifling side issue to be
> settled anyhow or anytime at the convenience of men.[28]

Political developments however were to bring the two groups closer together.

Solidarity

*One consolation Irishwomen, however, have and that is: the knowledge
that the most progressive of their country-men – who form the
majority – have stood by the Republican Proclamation of 1916 and
have given equal rights to men and women within and on the
Executive Committee of Sinn Fein.* [1]

On Easter Monday 1916 a combined force of Irish Volunteers
and Irish Citizen Army staged a rebellion in Dublin against the
British crown. Keypoints in the city were taken over, and from
the General Post Office in O'Connell Street (headquarters of
the insurgents) Padraic Pearse read the proclamation of the
provisional government of the Irish republic. The proclamation
was signed by Tom Clarke, Sean MacDiarmada, Thomas
MacDonagh, Padraic Pearse, Eamonn Ceannt, James Connolly
and Joseph Plunkett. It was addressed to Irishmen and
Irishwomen, and among its provisions it declared that:

> The Irish Republic is entitled to, and hereby claims, the
> allegiance of every Irishman and Irishwoman. The
> Republic guarantees religious and civil liberty, equal
> rights and equal opportunities to all its citizens and
> declares its resolve to pursue the happiness and
> prosperity of the whole nation and of all its parts,
> cherishing all the children of the nation equally.

The rebels held out until Saturday of that week, when they
were forced to surrender. Fifteen of their leaders were
subsequently executed, including all those who had signed the
proclamation. In the aftermath of the rebellion, and the
subsequent Sinn Fein victory at three by-elections (in north
Roscommon, east Clare, and south Longford) in 1917, the
British government decided to hold a national convention with
the aim of arriving at an agreed solution between Irishmen on
the future government of the island. Irish women sought
and were refused representation at the convention, which had
been boycotted by Sinn Fein and organised labour. [2] The *Irish*

Citizen editorial which is quoted above referred to the uncertain outcome of that convention, and sought to reassure Irish women on the grounds outlined. Examination of the facts, however, indicate that some Irish men had to be reminded of the provisions of the proclamation, which in its wording had taken account of the aspirations of suffrage and labour workers. Neither the proclamation nor the imminent passage of a British government bill giving votes to women over thirty ensured that the way was now clear for women's participation in public life. In April 1917 an All-Ireland conference was convened by Count Plunkett (winner of the by-election for Sinn Fein in Roscommon, and father of the executed Joseph Plunkett) to frame a national policy and to unite the various groups encompassed by Sinn Fein.[3] The IWFL was refused representation unless it abandoned its non-party stance and attended as a nationalist organisation. This the league refused to do, although some members attended in a private capacity as 'visitors'.[4] A number of nationalist women did, however, attend as delegates.

This Sinn Fein conference appointed a central steering committee of nine, of which one was a woman, Josephine Mary Plunkett. The following month, at the instigation of Inghinidhe na hEireann, women delegates held a conference of their own, in Dublin, in the home of Joseph Mary Plunkett in Fitzwilliam Street. (Not all the meetings were held in such comfortable surroundings, one being held in the bathroom adjoining the Round Room in Dublin's Mansion House in December 1917). In addition to the Inghinidhe, the conference was attended by representatives of the Cumann na mBan executive, the Irish Women Worker's Union, the women of the citizen Army.[5] Among the women in attendance at this or at subsequent meetings were Dr Kathleen Lynn, co-founder of St Ultan's Children's Hospital in Dublin in 1919; Aine Ceannt, an executive member of Cumann na mBan, widow of Eamonn Ceannt, signatory to the proclamation; Madeleine ffrench-Mullen, active with the ICA during the rising, and later co-founder of St Ultan's Hospital; Mabel FitzGerald, executive member of Cumann na mBan and mother of the present Taoiseach, Garrett FitzGerald Helena Molony, who in addition to her trade union activities had been an ICA member and had been imprisoned for her part in the rising; Marie Perolz, a native of Cork, member of the ICA and of Cumann na mBan; Kathleen Clarke from Limerick, another woman bereaved by the rising, who initiated the Volunteer dependants' fund (to aid the families of those imprisoned), and who in 1939 became the first woman Lord Mayor of Dublin. Others who attended meetings of the society included Louise Gavan Duffy, Alice Ginnell, Dulcibella Barton, Kitty O'Doherty, Winifred Carney, and Misses Kennedy, Shannon, Davis and Plunkett. Countess Plunkett outlined the proceedings of the council of nine on which she represented the interests of the women of Ireland. It was decided that the conference would be convoked again 'from time to time to discuss those subjects of importance to women which might arise'. This was to be more often than the women might have originally supposed. At that inaugural meeting, when the question of suffrage was raised, it was pointed out that Count Plunkett at the All-Ireland conference had taken his stand on the 1916 proclamation which granted equal rights to all citizens, men and women; 'such being the case there could be no talk of struggling for the vote after English or other methods, the vote had already been granted to Irishwomen by Irishmen'. The genuine extension of equal rights to women was not easily attained, however, and events were to prove that such extensions as occurred were not granted without a struggle.

Kathleen Lynn.

When the Sinn Fein committee of nine was reorganised and augmented to include released Sinn Fein prisoners and other factions of the nationalist movement, the women delegates sought increased representation. The women, in their letter to the Sinn Fein executive, stated tersely:

> The claim of women to be represented is based mainly on the Republican Proclamation of Easter week 1916, which, of course, you are determined to uphold.... The claim is also based on the risks women took, equally with the men, to have the Irish Republic established, on the necessity of having their organised co-operation in the further struggle to free Ireland, and the advantage of having their ideas on many social problems likely to arise in the near future. [6]

Their request was refused. The women considered sending a deputation to the Sinn Fein executive, but initially decided not to do this as 'Women have applied to them often enough and that the matter should be left for Cumann na mBan for the present to see what they could do'. [7] But Cumann na mBan had themselves been refused representation. Eventually the women delegates did form a deputation to the Sinn Fein executive which agreed to co-opt four women 'on the understanding that none of them represented any organisation, and that they be all members of a Sinn Fein branch' [8]. The four women co-opted were Aine Ceannt, Jennie Wyse Power, Miss Plunkett and Helena Moloney. The women's group put forward a resolution for recommendation by the Sinn Fein executive at a national convention to be held in October 1917. The text of their original resolution read:

> Whereas, according to the Republican Proclamation which guarantees 'religious and civil liberty, equal rights and equal opportunities to all its citizens', women are equally eligible with men as members of branches, members of the governing body and officers of both local and governing bodies, be it resolved:- that the equality of men and women in this organisation be emphasised in all

speeches, leaflets & pamphlets for the benefit of women hearers and readers who, so far, have had no politial training. [9]

Before the convention, the women considered circularising members already proposed for the new executive of Sinn Fein regarding their attitudes towards that paragraph in the republican proclamation referred to in their resolution. It was decided not to do so for fear that 'it would weaken our case to appear to think that there could be any doubt on the point' [10] After some changes, the women's resolution was accepted. The opening sentence now read 'whereas according to the rules of Sinn Fein and to the Republician Proclamation'...etc., while the concluding clause was changed to read: 'That the equality of men and women in this organisation be emphasised in all speeches and leaflets.' The amended final clause was adopted at the convention. Four women were elected to the new Sinn Fein Executive – Constance de Markievicz, Dr Kathleen Lynn, Kathleen Clarke, and Grace Plunkett. The *Irish Citizen* commented:

> We offer our hearty congratulations to the promoters and spokesmen of the Sinn Fein convention for the broad statesmanship and the public spirit they have displayed in endorsing and embodying in their new constitution, in the most unequivocal terms, the democratic principle of the complete equality of men and women in Ireland.

Nonetheless, the paper commented:

> It was regrettable to notice so few women delegates, an inequality which we strongly hope to see rectified on the occasion of future conventions. [11]

These were sentiments with which the women delegates were in complete agreement. At this stage they formally organised themselves into a society – Cumann na dTeachtaire – to consist of women delegates to all conferences held by Irish republicans. [12] Its constitution stated that the society was formed 'to watch the political movements in Ireland in the interests of Irishwomen'. The aims of the association were:

> to safe guard the political rights of Irishwomen
>
> to ensure adequate representation for them in the republican government
>
> to urge and facilitate the appointment of women to public boards throughout the country
>
> to educate Irish women in the rights and duties of citizenship

The association considered starting a women's paper, but because of the difficulties involved, decided to concentrate instead on producing occasional leaflets, and ensuring the publication of regular short articles giving women's point of view in as many local papers as possible. It also compiled lists of suitable women for appointment to local boards and committees. The Sinn Fein executive subsequently appointed some of their nominees to its various departments. In addition to considering women's role in the current political situation, Cumann na dTeachtaire also discussed other more mundane issues such as the scarcity of women's toilets in Dublin. Dr Kathleen Lynn, who was also director of public health for Sinn Fein, was directed to bring the matter before the proper corporation authorities. After consultation with the corporation, Dr Lynn reported a proposed scheme whereby selected paper shops throughout the city were to be registered as keeping a public toilet for women, and to put up a sign to that effect. The corporation was to bear the cost of installation and maintenance, and to provide an inspector (the association stipulated this must be a woman) where necessary. Participating shopkeepers were to be paid a suitable fee by the corporation for their services.[13] The constitution of the association advised that women delegates should be prepared to confer with other Irish women's societies:

> Whenever it can be accomplished without sacrifice of principle because they are convinced that the bringing

together of all Irishwomen to discuss matters of common interest on a neutral platform could not but be beneficial to all parties.[14]

This recommendation was indicative of a new co-operative atmosphere which developed between various women's groups after 1916. A combination of circumstances brought this about. The cumulative effect of the rebellion itself, the murder of Frank Sheehy Skeffington, the execution of republican leaders, followed by the mass imprisonment of republican activists, had a profound effect on the various women's organisations.

In 1916 Louie Bennett took over the running of both the Irish Womens Workers Union and the *Irish Citizen*, thereby strengthening the links between labour and suffrage supporters. The IWFL not only maintained its co-operation with labour, but developed a working partnership with nationalist women's organisations. Cumann na dTeachtaire and the IWFL were particularly close – some women, for example Jennie Wyse Power, Kathleen Lynn, Elizabeth Bloxham and Marian Duggan, being members of both societies. Even the IWSLGA had links with Cumann na dTeachtaire. Again there were instances of joint membership. Kathleen Lynn and Jennie Wyse Power were involved with both societies. When, following the passing of the Representation of the People Act in 1918 (which proposed extending the franchise to some women), a conference of all suffrage societies was organised in Dublin by the IWSLGA 'to consider the future with a view to possible amalgamation', Cumann na dTeachtaire decided to send delegates with instructions to withdraw 'should anything arise to compromise the society's political principles'.[15]

From 1916 a change is obvious in the *Irish Citizen* also. In addition to becoming a major source of information on the IWWU, an increasing number of its articles expressed nationalist sympathies. The paper gave its support to the demand for political status for republican prisoners, and as in the past, condemned the practise of forcible feeding. Both Cumann na dTeachtaire and the IWWU adopted St·Brigid as their patron, the former declaring that 'such a good suffragist should get recognition'.[16] Cumann na mBan was also to change after 1916, taking on a more active and aggressive role. Shortly after the rebellion it started its work on behalf of prisoners' dependants, with the objective of providing for the families of the men who were killed during the fight, as well as those interned and those deprived of employment. Brian Farrell has written of this work: 'In the absence of any other leadership in the later months of 1916... Prisoners Aid, largely managed by the women relatives of the executed men, became the spearhead of militant nationalism in Ireland'.[17] Shades of the Land League days! In February 1918 Cumann na dTeachtaire decided to co-opt as members of the association the executive of Cumann na mBan, and also to offer co-option 'to all women elected to public boards in the republican interest'[18]

This coming together of women's groups led to some notable instances of co-operation during 1918. One such issue was the anti-conscription campaign. During the war years the question of conscription had always been in the background. On the outbreak of war in 1914 Frank Sheehy Skeffington had written; 'The woman who does not... discourage recruiting has an imperfect understanding of the basis of the feminist movement.'[19] In 1915 Sylvia Pankhurst had written to Hanna Sheehy Skeffington warning her against 'industrial conscription' whereby women were persuaded to take men's jobs so that men could be released for fighting. Later that year the British Board of Trade actually sought the co-operation of the IWFL in publicising job vacancies for women for this precise reason.[20] The Labour Party and the *Irish Citizen* had consistently opposed conscription, industrial or military. In October 1916 the latter warned English women 'if conscription should be attemtped there is not a hamlet in Ireland but will resist it.... the women of Ireland will not tolerate the taking away by force of their men-kind.'[21] In the spring of 1918 the Conscription Act was extended to Ireland. The Irish Parliamentary Party voted against the measure and returned to Ireland in protest at its passage. In the massive revolt of the Irish public against the Act women played a major role. The IWFL described the act as 'an imperative call to action for the militants.'[22]

Representatives of Labour and Sinn Fein, parliamentarians and others gathered together in a conference which declared that Ireland was a separate and disinct nation entitled to self-determination.[23] On 21 April 1918 two million men and women signed a pledge to resist conscription, and the following week at a mass meeting of women in the Mansion House in Dublin, Cumann na mBan, the IWFL and other women's organisations made a similar pledge 'all the women present standing and repeating it aloud, hands uplifted.'[24] Labour too organised its protest – a national one-day strike on 23 April 1918, effective everywhere except Belfast. On this day a banner was hung from the offices of the IWFL which read:

CONSCRIPTION – No woman must take a man's job.[25]

On 9 June 1918 a national women's day was held, during which women throughout the country pledged not to take jobs vacated by men being conscripted. In Dublin the signing of this pledge took place in City Hall, to which representatives of various women's societies marched in procession. The *Irish Citizen* declared:

> The call to the women of Ireland to solemnly pledge themselves against the taking of posts vacated through the enforced military service of their countrymen has been nobly answered. Through the length and breadth of the land their voices have been raised to heaven in united supplication that their country be spared the devastating tyranny of conscription.[26]

Their prayers – and their actions – were noted, and the Conscription Act was not applied in Ireland.

In many ways the post-1916 wave of nationalism which swept the country submerged the women's groups, the IWFL reporting in 1918 that:

> The passing of the Conscription Act and the militarist reign of terror then inaugurated rendered the carrying on of suffrage activities impossible, and from this time forward all the energies of the League were diverted into

Anti-Conscription propaganda.[27]

The other major issue on which women's groups co-operated was the campaign against venereal disease and the related implementation of Regulation 40 D. under the Defence of the Realm Act (DORA). The concern of women's groups about the question of VD had been evident in the pages of the *Irish Citizen* for some time past. Dublin presented a particular problem. Arthur Griffith had drawn attention to British Army medical reports which confirmed that there was a higher incidence of VD among soldiers in Dublin than elsewhere in the United Kingdom.[28] In March 1918 Cumann na dTeachtaire organised a conference of women's societies to consider 'the serious menace of venereal disease in Dublin,' their minutes noting that 'this was a matter on which women of every shade of political opinion could unite in order to discuss the best measures to be adopted to combat this evil.'[29] All Irish women doctors and representatives of the Irish Nurses Association were also invited. When planning their conference, Cumann na dTeachtaire conferred with the IWSLGA who were organising a second conference of the combined suffrage societies, so that the two conferences might be held on consecutive days to facilitate the attendance of members at both. A further indication of co-operation emerged when Margaret Connery of the IWFL was chosen by Cumann na dTeachtaire to chair their conference in place of Jennie Wyse Power, who had been called to Waterford to assist in the by-election. Ten women's groups were represented at the conference, and messages of support were received from eighteen others. A committee of the various societies was formed, and a resolution was passed at the conference and sent to the corporations of Dublin and Belfast.[30]

The implementation of Regulation 40 D DORA in August 1918 further infuriated women. This regulation introduced 'to safeguard the health of soldiers' was denounced by the *Irish Citizen* as an attempt to revive the notorious Contagious Diseases Acts, which had been repealed in 1886 after years of strenuous agitation by Irish and English Suffragists. Under the terms of Regulation 40, any woman could be arrested by the police 'on suspicion,' and detained until proved innocent by a medical examination. A woman could also be handed over to the police on a verbal charge made by a soldier. The *Irish Citizen* pointed out that compulsory examination of women had been proved to be a futile safeguard, and in fact increased the danger of disease by giving men a false sense of security, while it 'constituted an outrage on the honour and self-respect of women, and is the gravest possible menance to their individual

MAY, 1913.]   THE LEPRACAUN.   151

When she gets it, what will she do with it?

Cartoon from *The Lepracaun* 1913.

liberty.'[31] In August 1918 the paper reported the first case in Ireland under the Act – that of a Belfast woman given six months hard labour 'for communicating disease' to a Canadian soldier. The paper concluded that the real object of the regulation was 'to make the practice of vice safe for men by degrading and befouling women.' Again, women's groups organised to protest against what the IWFL termed 'the state regulation of vice.' The League, while determined that every effort should be made to prevent the spread of VD, deplored the one-sided and discriminatory nature of this regulation. A very active publicity campaign was embarked on, with flag displays warning women of the dangers, public meetings of protest and letters to the press, which were published only by the *The Voice of Labour,* the Labour Newspaper.[32]

Despite these two major incidences of active co-operation between women's groups, old political differences emerged. Thus the IWSLGA was active in the campaign against VD, but not in the anti-recruitment campaign. Nonetheless, co-operation between women's groups during 1918 was at its highest since 1912. In their emphasis on promoting the political education of women, legislation for the benefit of women, the election of women to government, local boards, councils and all public offices, all these organisations shared similar basic objectives. 1918 proved a watershed for the women's movement in Ireland on two counts – firstly, legislation of that year gave the parliamentary vote to some women, thereby partly achieving the primary aim of suffrage groups while removing the one goal common to all. Secondly, and more importantly in the Irish context, the results of that general election in 1918, in which women were to play a crucial role, confirmed the political incompatibility of the various groups. So the IWFL, reporting on the series of meetings held by the IWSLGA with a view to future amalgamation, stated: 'Owing to the disturbed state of the political atmosphere no common basis of agreement could be arrived at.'[33]

From a feminist viewpoint the formation of Cumann na dTeachtaire is most significant, and is a clear indication of unease among committed nationalist women about their role in the new Ireland. Later events were to prove that their unease was not unfounded. Unfortunately, by then these women, like their male counterparts, had been divided politically, and the possibility of a potentially, effective women's movement in the new state diminished.

Cartoon from *Votes for Women* 1912.

Victory – The Vote

Women have very little to hope for from political revolutions. Social revolutions offered an opportunity for reforms which go nearer to the heart of things and affect the lives of women more closely than mere political revolutions. [1] Margaret Connery

In January 1918 the Representation of the People Act granted the parliamentary vote to women of thirty years of age and over. The vote was also extended to men of twenty-one years. This age provision avoided the immediate establishment of a female majority in the electorate. [2] That the bill was extended to Ireland was not due to a sudden conversion on the part of Irish politicians. On the contrary, attempts were made to postpone the extension of the bill to Ireland, with the Irish Parliamentary Party passing a resolution to this effect, and the executive of the Irish County Councils General Council stating that this was a question to be dealt with by an Irish parliament. Similar pressure was also brought to bear by unionist politicians. Both they and members of the Irish Parliamentary Party feared the effect of an increased electorate in the next general election – justifiably as subsequent events proved.

While the *Irish Citizen* was later to call for the removal of 'the odious age-restriction', deeming it as great an insult as total disfranchisement, for the moment is rejoiced that at last the sex barrier was broken. Suffragists were advised to work unitedly to 'secure the speedy emancipation of those women still outside the pale.' [3] Despite its limitations, the francise extension initially created a demand for more female involvement in national affairs. The *Irish Citizen* reported that women were much in demand as speakers on party platforms, and noted the disappearance of advertisements such as those formerly published by the Irish Parliamentary Party reading 'Public admitted – ladies excluded'. [4] The Labour Party was the first to nominate a woman candidate for the general election of 1918 – Louie Bennett – although she declined the invitation. William O'Brien, Chairman at the 1918 Trades Union Congress in Waterford, discussing the new voters on the register, declared that 'chief among them are the women, our sisters in many a good fight...means must now be found to associate the women

with us in our political as well as in our industrial work.'[5] Sinn
Fein also sought the support of the new women voters.
Referring to the mother of the late Padraic Pearse, Irish women
were asked in an election pamphlet to 'save Ireland by voting as
MRS PEARSE will vote', with the promise that 'as in the past, so
in the future the womenfolk of the Gael shall have high place in
the Councils of a freed Gaelic nation,'[6] The fulfilment of such
promises, however, proved hard to obtain. Even before the
election there were indications that all was not well. At the last
Sinn Fein convention, two resolutions had been proposed
stating that no candidate would be selected where a
parliamentary vacancy occurs 'other than a man who took part
in the fight of Easter Week.'[7] While this may have been moved
with by-elections in mind, the sexist tone of the
recommendation is worthy of note, particularly when one
considers that at this same conference the resolution regarding
the equality of men and women in the organisation was
adopted. When the precise question of women candidates for
the 1918 general election was raised, the Sinn Fein standing
committee vacillated 'on whether it would be according to
law.'[8] In the event, Sinn Fein alone ran women candidates, and
then only two – Constance de Markievicz in Dublin and
Winifred Carney in Belfast. The *Irish Citizen* commented that 'it
looks as if Irishmen (even Republicans) need teaching in this
matter'.[9]

Women in fact played a crucial role in this election, both as
voters and as party workers. This was acknowledged by Sinn
Fein in their request that Hanna Sheehy Skeffington should be
a 'woman speaker' in their victory celebrations in Pembroke
electoral division, in the Ballsbridge/Donnybrook area of
Dublin, 'in view of the fact that the women voters were the most
important factor in our polling district.'[10] In addition to the
Sinn Fein landslide victory of that election there occurred
another victory of particular delight for Irish women. Although
she never took her seat, Constance de Markievicz became the
first female M P elected to the British parliament. Commenting
on the election results the IWFL in its report for 1918 stated:

an element of ironic justice in the fact that women, whose
claims it so long opposed with such unbending hostility,
should have played so large a part in its final annihilation.
Under the new dispensation the majority sex in Ireland
has secured one representative. This is the measure of our
boasted sex equality. The lesson the election teaches is
that reaction has not died out with the Irish Party – and
the IWFL which has been so faithful to feminist ideals,
must continue to fight and expose reaction in the future as
in the past.[11]

Cumann na dTeachtaire members argued that women had
neglected their opportunities at the general election, claiming
that had a list of suitable women candidates been presented to
all Sinn Fein selection committees the women of Ireland would
have achieved more equitable representation in Dail Eireann
(lower house of the Irish Parliament).[12] Bearing in mind the
attitude of the Sinn Fein executive it would seem that more
extreme action would have been required, and even that not necessarily proving more effective. This sense of disillusionment
continued during 1920 with the publication of the numbers of
women elected to local councils. The *Irish Independent,* reporting
on the local government elections held early in 1920,
commented that 'a fair proportion of women' had been elected.
The *Irish Citizen* retorted that five in eighty of Dublin city
council or forty-two in the whole country scarcely resembled a
'fair proportion.'[13] Another cause of unease to the *Irish Citizen*
was the increasing incidence of women being appointed to
public boards and positions primarily because of their
republican connections.

1918, therefore, saw the partial attainment of suffrage
objectives and a changing approach to women who could now
not only be party workers, but candidates and, above all, voters.
Around the world many feminist and socialist movements had
disintegrated under the impact of war. Where suffrage groups
survived they faded away once the vote was achieved, their
raison d'etre removed. The tenuous coalition of women of
differing political views was no longer necessary and women's
solidarity split on party lines. While most Irish suffrage societies
remained intact during and after the war, increasingly the

energies of suffragists were drawn into the political struggles of the day. In 1920 Hanna Sheehy Skeffington wrote

> Since 1912, that is for eight long and difficult years half the time being consumed in a world war, the *Irish Citizen* has championed the cause of woman's emancipation.... In Ireland at present we are in a state of war, and all the conditions prevailing in other countries during the late European War now apply at home. Just as then the woman's movement became patriots' or heroes' wives or widows, rather than human beings, so now in Ireland the national struggle overshadows all else.... There can be no woman's paper without a woman's movement, without earnest and serious minded women readers and thinkers and these have dwindled perceptively of late, partly owing to the cause above mentioned and partly because since a measure, however limited, of suffrage has been granted women are forging out their own destiny in practical fields of endeavour.... We still believe that we have a mission and a message for Irishwomen as a purely feminist paper and emboldened in that belief we shall carry on. [14]

Unfortunately, shortly afterwards the *Irish Citizen* was forced to close down when a member of the British Forces smashed its press.

Suffragists had always maintained that possession of the parliamentary vote would give women the power to influence government, and the role of Irish women voters in 1918 proved that point to the detriment of the Irish Parliamentary Party. That influence – or fear of that influence – was very real in the early days of the new Irish state. Adult suffrage had been included in the 1916 proclamation, and in the spirit of that proclamation, was included in the Irish Free State constitution of 1922, under whose provisions all citizens of twenty-one years were enfranchised. It is in this provision, rather than in the 1918 act, that the influence of Irish women – suffragists and labour – can principally be seen. Even still, franchise extension was not obtained without a final struggle. At the time of the treaty discussions held in London in 1921 in an attempt to resolve the question of Irish independence, Hanna Sheehy Skeffington led a deputation to Griffith and de Valera stressing the need for consideration of women's views on the subject. Marie Johnson recorded that Griffith was most ungracious, but that de Valera, 'more suave, more inclined to placate, seized the chance to agree, realising that it meant well to have intelligent women on his side agreed to all our requests for full citizenship.'[15] During the acrimonious treaty debates of the second Dail in 1922, the issue of women's suffrage received heated discussion.[16]. Unlike previous situations where there had been a clear pro and anti-women's suffrage lobby, now both sides proclaimed their allegiance to the provisions of the 1916 proclamation. As of old, however, the women's vote was seen as a pawn in the game of power. Pro and anti-treaty representatives both claimed that the majority of Irish women favoured their side, although it would appear that, as in 1918 when John Redmond had feared the effect of a new female electorate, now the pro-treaty side had precisely such a fear of enfranchising women under thirty. Ultimately suffrage for adults over twenty-one years was introduced in the Free State constitution of 1922, and can be seen as the last piece of progresive legislation affecting women until recent times.

Where women attempted to play a role in the moulding of the new Irish state, their actions were criticised by those of differing political opinion. So we find P S O'Hegarty in 1924 criticising Dr Ada English for deciding to vote with the other women members of the second Dail January 1922 against the treaty, rather than pro-treaty as she had originally intended. He denounces her comment that 'all the women should stand together' and her subsequent vote as a 'sex vote'.[17] He describes as 'useful and constructive' the work done by Inghinidhe na hEireann, that society never forgetting that there was special work it could do which men could not, 'just as it never forgot that it could not and should not do men's work.' He compares this with the role played later by Cummann na mBan, criticising that organisation's militarist attitude, stating that 'Woman's business in the world is with the things of life...but these women busied themselves with nothing but the things of death.' He tells us that during the civil war 'Dublin was full of hysterical women,' who never tried to understand the political situation, but jumped to conclusions without any consideration except their emotions. He concludes that:

> Left to himself, man is comparatively harmless. He will always exchange smokes and drinks and jokes with his enemy, and he will always pity the 'poor devil' and wish that the whole business was over... It is woman... with her implacability, her bitterness, her hysteria, that makes a devil of him. The Suffragettes used to tell us that with women in political power there would be no more war. We know that with women in political power there would be no more peace.

Were women in political power? Maurice Manning has written that as far as the political rights and constitutional status of women were concerned, the new Irish state of 1922 was all that might be desired. Irishwomen had in fact beaten Englishwomen to the vote – it was not until 1928 that the vote was extended to all English women. Manning notes, however, that:

> the new regime quickly discarded the radical rhetoric and revolutionary flourishes of the 1916-21 period and settled into a conservative and respectable state – a state which put a high emphasis on law and order, on the maintenance of the current economic orthodoxies and on social caution. [18]

He points out that nowhere was this social caution more clearly reflected than in the attitudes of the entire community to the question of women in politics. In 1952, thirty years after independence there were fewer women in elected politics than in 1922 and their impact and effectiveness was undoubtedly less. Writing in the late 1970s, Manning states that women TDs (elected representatives) always placed party before sex, working hard in the interests of their constituents, but knowing their place in a male-dominated political world – and keeping to it. He deduces that since the electors kept sending the same women back to the Dail, that this is presumably what they wanted.

While technically the campaign for women's suffrage can be counted a success, in that its primary aim of votes for women was achieved, the related objective of complete equality for women in all spheres of life was not. Suffragists such as Hanna Sheehy Skeffington and Margaret Cousins had looked upon attainment of the vote as one step in the creation of a society wherein women would be accorded equality in opportunity and rights, becoming active and involved citizens. In 1919 the editorial of the *Irish Citizen* demanded:

> We want equal pay for equal work, equal marriage laws, the abolition of legal disabilities, the right of women to enter the hitherto banned learned professions, women jurors and justices, in short, the complete abolition of various taboos and barriers – social, economic and political – that still impede women's progress and consequently that of the race.[19]

The decades that followed Irish independence were to show how far from attainment was this ideal, the constitution of 1937 actually regressing the position of women rather than improving it. Some women sought to correct that situation. A number of women's groups, including ex-suffragists, came together in 1937 in opposition to certain articles in the proposed new constitution which implied curtailment of the unequivocal equality of status and opportunity granted under Article 3 of the Free State constitution. These women were concerned that 'the proposed constitution leaves the door open for reactionary legislation against women in every department'. These groups, however, represented a minority of Irish women, and no effective women's movement emerged at that time. While political events undoubtedly impeded the emergence of an active women's movement in the new state, another significant factor must have been the acceptance by the majority of women of their secondary status. An *Irish Citizen* article in 1917 highlighted a key weakness in the attitude of Irish women:

All that is best amongst you holds to the feminist ideal, yet many of you stand aloof from feminism because of the political movement.... But you have not justified your abstention from the women's struggle for liberty by becoming a force within the new movement, and there demonstrating your human equality. You are but clinging to the outward fringe. Believe me, you wrong your womanhood and your country by such feebleness... You are in revolt against a subjection imposed from without, but you are tacitly acquiescing in a position of inferiority within.

It concluded in what today can be seen as a prophetic way:

If in the course of time the new national movement becomes wholly masculine and stereotyped for lack of the humaness of outlook which women's presence and full co-operation would supply, you cannot escape your share of responsibility for such a disastrous state of things. If you leave men alone to carry out the task of national creative endeavour, you will have no right to complain later that there are flaws in construction; and there will be flaws, grave and serious flaws, if the women of Ireland fail to demand and take their full women's share in the national heritage. [20]

The sublimation of women's issues to controversial national questions ensured that the position of Irish women remained subservient, a situation compounded by the deepening Catholic ethos of the state. The depressed status of women in Ireland reflected the conservative values of Irish society, which, as Mary E Daly points out, was reinforced by the absence of any strong impetus for change. [21] Despite the efforts of some of the old gang; of the suffrage era, who strove throughout their lives to reform the position of women in Irish society, no effective women's movement emerged in the new state. The prevailing ethos of the time placed emphasis on the family unit, not on individual rights. Describing the status of women in 1930 as a 'sorry travesty of emancipation,' Helena Molony advised women and the labour movement to review their objectives and policy in the light of Connolly's writings:

> Women, since his day, have got that once coveted right to vote, but they still have their inferior status, their lower pay for equal work, their exclusion from juries and certain branches of the civil service, their slum dwellings, and crowded, cold and unsanitary schools for their children. [22]

The principal reason that the broader objectives of the suffrage movement were not achieved, and that the travesty of emancipation occurred instead, lies chiefly in the absence of a feminist perspective in Irish society generally, until comparatively recent times. While there had been committed and articulate feminists in Ireland, particularly from 1910 onwards, they were at all times a minority group. As has been shown, many women who held feminist views chose to subjugate them for party political reasons, unlike such idealists as Hanna Sheehy Skeffington, who maintained such views over and above political considerations. The tragedy is that in subjugating their feminist ambitions, they ultimately sacrificied them. While thousands of women flocked to join Cumann na mBan after the 1916 rising and played a crucial role in political developments over the next decade, it should be remembered that the majority of such women did so for nationalist, not feminist reasons. The mass of Irishwomen were untouched by feminism.

This was not just an Irish phenonemon. Maurice Manning has shown that after suffrage was granted in the US, women's groups suffered, partly because of a general swing to the right, but also because of the indifference of the mass of women voters, who usually voted the same as their husbands. [23] In Ireland, a tradition of party political loyalty was compounded by the social, economic and religious values of the state. The great majority of Irish women did not question their role in the new Ireland.

Suffragists would have argued that women disregarded what could have been their most effective weapon in achieving equality – their vote. While the vote could be a useful weapon in achieving their objectives through the election of politicians committed to reform, it would not in itself guarantee change. An examination of the role and status of women in Irish society from 1922 up to the 1970s would confirm that. The desire for such change must come from within. Only then can a woman's vote be effective for a woman.

To the modern eye some of the early campaigners perhaps appear naive in their expectation that women, having the vote, would inevitably change society and improve the condition of women. To those women, however, and to many other groups excluded from voting for reasons of sex, age or class, the vote was a relatively new instrument in the exercise of parliamentary democracy. The fact that it was withheld from them for so long and so jealously guarded as the preserve of one sex made its attainment all the more desirable. If in the next general election voting rights were restricted to one sex, we might come near to the feelings of women sixty-six years ago.

Votes for women, however, was but one issue in the demands of the early feminist movement. Its leaders would be heartened to see the development of a further phase of Irish feminism and the development – however shakily – of a feminist perspective in Irish society. With the significant societal changes in the country over the past two decades, the restructuring of society sought by the pioneers of the women's movement may be achieved. Irish women can be proud of the dedicated women who attempted in their lifetime to achieve this ideal. Their memory can best be honoured by completing the task they started.

Notes

Seeds of Unrest

1 Edward Gibson, 'The Employment of Women in Ireland', *Statistical and Social Inquiry Society of Ireland* (Dublin 1863) vol. III.

2 R. J. Evans, *The Feminists: Women's Emancipation Movements in Europe, America and Australasia, 1840-1920* (London 1977) p. 34.

3 Peter Murray, 'Electoral Politics and the Dublin Working Class Before the First World War', *Saothar* 6, (Journal of the Irish Labour History Society)1980, p. 9.

4 H. Blackburn, *A Record of the Women's Suffrage Movement in the British Isles* (London 1902).

5 Andrew Rosen, *Rise Up Women! The Militant Campaign of the Women's Social and Political Union 1903-1914* (London and Boston 1974) p.5.

6 Ruth Dudley Edwards, *An Atlas of Irish History* (London 1973) p.214.

7 J. J. Lee, 'Women and the Church since the Famine', *Women in Irish Society, The Historical Dimension* (Arlen House, Dublin 1978) p.38.

8 ibid.

9 Mary E. Daly, 'Women in the Irish Workforce from Pre-Industrial to Modern Times', *Saothar* 7 (Journal of the Irish Labour History Society) 1981, p.75.

10 Lee op. cit. p.43.

11 Margaret MacCurtain, 'Towards an Appraisal of the Religious Image of Women' in *The Crane Bag* 4, no. 1, 1980, p.29.

12 Daly op. cit. p.76.

13 Lee op. cit. p.39.

14 Eibhlin Breathnach, 'A History of the Movement for Women's Higher Education in Dublin 1860-1912', unpublished MA thesis, University College Dublin, 1981.

15 Lee op. cit.

16 ibid. pp 41-42.

The Awakening

1 'Womanhood and its Mission', *Dublin University Magazine part I* (Dublin 1859) p.628.

2 J. Mill, article on 'Government' in *Encyclopaedia Britanica,* Supplement to 4th, 5th and 6th editions, vol. 4 (1820) p.500.

3 The British and Irish Ladies Society for improving the condition and promoting the industry and welfare of the Female Peasantry in Ireland, *Annual Reports 1823-28.*

4 *Englishwoman's Journal* vol. no. 1 (1858) pp 332-338; 3 (1859) pp.357-8; vol. no. 9-10 (1862-63) pp 30-40.

5 *Irish Citizen* 21 March 1914.

6   *Englishwoman's Journal* 8 (1862) pp 226-9.

7   H. Blackburn op. cit. pp.53-56; also *Reports of the Irish Women's Suffrage and Local Government Association 1896-1918* (IWSLGA), preface to report for 1918.

8   *Irish Citizen* 25 May 1912.

9   Blackburn op. cit. p.140.

10 *Dublin University Magazine,* Part II (Dublin 1859) p.699.

11 J. S. Mill to Thomas Haslam 17 August 1867, Library of Society of Friends, Eustace Street, Dublin.

12 John Walter Bourke, *The Emancipation of Women* (contained in a volume of women's suffrage pamphlets 1871-80, Fawcett Library, London, ref. 396.11).

13 *IWSLGA Annual Reports* op. cit.

14 E. Garvey, *The Position of Irishwomen in Local Administration* (leaflet published for the Women's Emancipation Union 1896).

15 Ian d'Alton, 'Southern Irish Unionism' in *Transactions of the Royal Historical Society,* 5th series, 23, 1973, p.85; also R. Fulford, *Votes for Women* (London 1957) p.94.

16 Rosen op. cit. p.12.

17 *IWSLGA, Annual Report 1918* (preface).

18 *Irish Citizen* 21 March 1914.

19 For a detailed study of the Ladies' Land League see Margaret Ward, *Unmanageable Revolutionaries, Women and Irish Nationalism* (Brandon, Dingle 1983).

20 House of Commons Debates (H.C. Deb.), 4s, 37, 18 February 1896, p.631.

21 H.L.Deb., 4s, 37, 2 March 1896, p. 1450.

22 H.C.Deb., 4s, 45, 3 February 1897, pp 1202/1220.

23 H.C.Deb., 4s, 57, 12 May 1898, pp 1099/1103-1104.

24 Eibhlin Breathnach, 'Women and Higher Education in Ireland (1879-1914)', *The Cranebag* 1980, p.48.

25 IWSLGA *Annual Report 1903,* p.7.

Irishwomen Unite

1   J. H. and M. E. Cousins, *We Two Together* (Madras, India 1950) p.150.

2   *Irish Freedom,* October 1913.

3   Mary Colum, *Life and the Dream* (New York 1947) p.153 and p.174.

4   Hanna Sheehy Skeffington, 'Reminiscences of an Irish Suffragette', *Votes for Women, Irish Women's Struggle for the Vote* (Dublin 1975) (edited and published by A. D. Sheehy Skeffington and Rosemary Owens) p.12.

5   E. Pankhurst, *My Own Story* (London 1914) p.18.

6   Cousins op. cit. p.164. op. cit. also Cousins op. cit. p.164.

7   The *Irish Citizen* 25 May 1912 gives membership as 'over 1000'. The 1913 annual report of the IWFL states that there were 828 members and associates, with subscribers to various projects and funds bringing numbers up to 1016. This would indicate that the IWFL had the largest membership among Irish suffrage societies. Later reports do not give membership details.

8   Cousins op. cit. p.185.

9   *Irish Citizen* 7 May 1913.

10   *IWSF Reports 1912-14;* also *Irish Citizen* 17 June 1914.

11   Cousins op. cit. p.185.

12   Hanna Sheehy Skeffington, Reminiscences, op. cit. p.14.

13   L. M. McCraith, 'Irishwomen and their Vote', *New Ireland Review,* 30, (December 1908) pp 197-8.

14   *The Leader* 19 March 1910.

15   Rev. D. Barry S.T.L., 'Female Suffrage from a Catholic Standpoint', *Irish Ecclesiastical Record,* 4s, 26 (September 1909), pp 295-303.

16   *Bean na hEireann* 1909-11.

17   *Irish Citizen* 1912-20. The paper was a weekly until 1916, when it became a monthly paper.

18   A. Birrell to J. Dillon 15 January 1912 Trinity College Dublin (TCD), Dillon papers, MS 6799, item 182 a .

19   Hanna Sheehy Skeffington, Reminiscences, op. cit. p.18.

20   Pamphlet issued by the National Union of Women's Suffrage Societies, (Fawcett Library, London, ref. 396.11). The NUWSS were so impressed that they had the speeches of both men published as a pamphlet.

21   Rosen op. cit. pp 11, 67, 97.

22   Letter to Arthur Balfour from Lady Constance Lytton 1 June 1911 (Balfour papers British Museum MS 49793, vol.CXI, p.160). Lady Lytton's brother was chairman of the conciliation committee.

23   Rosen op. cit. p.154.

24   *Irish Citizen* 25 May 1912.

25   Letter reprinted in the *Irish Citizen* 3 August 1912.

26   *Freeman's Journal* 1 April 1912.

27   ibid. 18 April 1912.

28   *Irish Citizen* 8 June 1912.

29   *Irish Citizen* 8 and 15 June 1912; this composite reference covers the following three extracts quoted.

30   ibid. 22 June 1912.

Action and Reaction

1   Hanna Sheehy Skeffington, Reminiscences, p.18.

2   *Irish Times* 14 June 1912.

3   *Irish Citizen* 22 June 1912.

4   Sheehy Skeffington papers, National Library of Ireland (NLI), MS 21195.
5   *Irish Citizen* 6 July 1912.
6   *Evening Telegraph* 8 July 1912.
7   ibid. 9 July 1912.
8   ibid. 8 July 1912.
9   *Irish Citizen* 27 July 1912; also G. Dangerfield, *The Strange Death of Liberal England* (3rd edition, London 1970) pp 169-70.
10 *Evening Herald* 19 July 1912; also *Evening Telegraph* 19 July 1912.
11 State Paper Office of Ireland (SPO), CSO, Police and Crime Reports 1886-1914, carton 4.
12 *Irish Independent* 20 July 1912; *Evening Herald* 19 July 1912.
13 ibid.; details in this paragraph regarding mob violence against women can also be found in *Saturday Herald* 20 July 1912, the *Irish Citizen* 27 July 1912, and Hanna Sheehy Skeffington, Reminiscences, p.22.
14 K. Tynan, *The Years of the Shadow* (London 1919) p.109.
15 *Irish Independent* 29 July 1912.
16 *The Leader* 3 August 1912.
17 *Irish Citizen* 6 September 1913.
18 *Evening Telegraph* 7 August 1912; *Irish Citizen* 10 August 1912.

19 Rosen op. cit. p.143.
20 C. Pankhurst, *Unshackled* (London 1959) p.224.
21 *Sinn Féin* 17 August 1912.
22 ibid. 24 August 1912.

23 Hanna Sheehy Skeffington, Reminiscences, p. 23.
24 A. Birrell to J. Dillon 15 August 1912 (Dillon papers, TCD).
25 SPO, General Prisons' Board, Suffragette Papers 1912-14, box 1.
26 ibid.
27 ibid, boxes 1-3.

28 *Irish Citizen* 29 March and 26 April 1913.
29 *Irish Citizen* 5 July 1913.
30 *Irish Citizen* 13 July and 2 November 1912, and 17 May 1913; Hanna Sheehy Skeffington, Reminiscences, pp 24 and 26; *Irish Women's Suffrage Federation, Annual Report* 1912–13.

31 Cousins, op.cit. pp 189-90.
32 Hanna Sheehy Skeffington, Reminiscences, op. cit.
33 *Irish Citizen* 27 July 1912.
34 Hanna Sheehy Skeffington, Reminiscences, p.17.
35 *Church of Ireland Gazette* 29 May 1914.
36 *Irish Citizen* 13 September 1913.
37 Sheehy Skeffington papers, NLI, MS 22664.

38 | Date | Place | Object | Estimated Value |
| --- | --- | --- | --- |
| 27 March | Belfast | Abbeylands (residence) | £20,000. |
| 10 April | " | Orlands Mansion | several thousand |
| 16 " | Derry | House | £500. |
| 18 " | Belfast | Tea House | several thousand. |
| 22 " | " | Annadale House | £500. |
| 3 May | " | Pavillion | £500. |
| 3 July | Co. Down | Ballymenoch House | £20,000. |
| 29 July | Newtownards | Race Stand | £750. |

(Rosen op. cit. pp 229-42).

39 Crown solicitor to under secretary 5 August 1914, (SPO, CSORP, 13437).

Labour Link

1 J. Connolly, *The Re-conquest of Ireland* (Dublin 1917) p.291.
2 *Irish Citizen* 27 September 1913.
3 ibid. 7 February 1914.
4 ibid. 2 and 9 August, 1913; also 6 December, 1913. For more detailed examination of the interaction between labour and suffrage workers see R. Owens, 'Votes for Ladies, Votes for Women, Organised Labour and the Suffrage Movement, 1876-1922', *Saothar* 9, 1983, pp 32-47.
5 *Irish Citizen* 4 January 1913.
6 *Bean na hÉireann* March 1910.
7 Dermot Keogh, *The Rise of the Irish Working Class* (Belfast 1982) p. 179.
8 C. Desmond Greaves, *The Irish Transport and General Workers' Union – The Formative Years, 1909-1923* (Dublin 1982) p.64.
9 *Irish Worker* 9 September 1911. In Belfast Mary Galway had already organised some women workers in the Textile Operatives Society. Attempts to organise other women workers in the mills in co-operation with the ITGWU were opposed by Mary Galway and Jim Larkin. See Owens, art. cit.
10 *Irish Citizen* 6 September 1913.
11 ibid. 20 September 1913
12 *Irish Worker* 30 November 1912.
13 *Worker's Republic* 18 December 1915.
14 R. M. Fox, *Louie Bennett, her Life and Times* (Dublin 1957) p.63; *Irish Citizen* April 1917; *IWFL Report 1916*.
15 *Irish Citizen* January 1918.
16 ibid. November 1919.
17 ibid. January 1920.
18 ibid. December 1919.
19 Charles McCarthy, *Trade Unions in Ireland 1894-1960* (Dublin 1977) p.150.

20   *Report of Commission on Vocational Organisation* (Dublin 1943) para 294.
21   *Irish Citizen* October 1917.
22   *Irish Times* 28 February 1919.
23   *Irish Citizen* January 1920.
24   ibid. November 1918.
25   ibid. June 1912.
26   *ITUC Report for 1912,* p.52.
27   Hanna Sheehy Skeffington, Reminiscences, op. cit. p.17.
28   *ITUC Report for 1914,* pp 77–79.
29   Memoirs of Marie Johnson in Sheehy Skeffington papers, NLI, MS 21194(1).
30   *Irish Citizen* 28 December 1912.
31   ibid. 13 November 1913.
32   *ITUC Report for 1913,* pp 66–7.
33   Rosen op. cit. pp 218 and 223.
34   Correspondence of Henry Devinish Harben 1912–14, British Museum, MS 58226, No.57.
35   *Irish Worker* 4 April 1914.
36   Harben op. cit.
37   Francis Sheehy Skeffington to Mrs Baker 20 March 1914, in Sheehy Skeffington papers, NLI MS 21634 (XVI).
38   *Irish Citizen* 7 February 1914.
39   ibid.
40   ibid. July 1917.
41   ibid. February 1920.
42   ibid. October 1919.
43   R. M. Fox, *Rebel Irishwomen* (Dublin 1967) pp 75-6.
44   Helena Molony, 'James Connolly and Women', *Dublin Labour Year Book, 1930* (James Connolly Commemoration) p.32.
45   *Irish Citizen* 23 October 1915.
46   ibid. July 1918.

Splinters of War

  1   *Irish Citizen* 15 August 1914.
  2   ibid, 22 August, 26 September, 17 October 1914; Rosen op. cit. pp 248-9 and 252-4.
  3   *IWSLGA Reports 1914 and 1915;* also SPO, CSORP, 2654 (1915).
  4   *Irish Citizen* 15 August 1914; the paper claimed that a letter in connection with the formation of the council was refused publication by the *Irish Times* and *Irish Independent,* but was published by the *Freeman's Journal.*
  5   *IWSF Annual Report 1913-14;* also, minutes of IWSF executive committee, 15 August 1914 and 13 March 1915, Sheehy

Skeffington papers, NLI, MS 21196.

6   *Irish Citizen* 21 November 1914.
7   ibid. 19 September 1914.
8   Sheehy Skeffington papers, NLI, MS 22667 (ii).
9   C. Pankhurst op. cit. p.288.
10   *Irish Citizen* 12 September 1914.
11   ibid. 19 September 1914.
12   P.H. Pearse to Hanna Sheehy Skeffington 9 May 1915 (NLI, Women's Suffrage Exhibition materials, MS 21194-21197).
13   *Irish Citizen* 22 May 1915.
14   ibid.
15   ibid.; this was later reprinted and published as a pamphlet.
16   ibid. 27 February 1915.
17   ibid. 29 August 1914.

Suffrage First Before All Else

1   Constance de Markievicz, *Women, Ideals and the Nation* (Inghinidhe na hEireann, Dublin 1909) p.4.
2   *Irish Citizen* 1 March 1913.
3   Cousins op. cit. p.164.
4   Press cutting of letter from Agnes O'Farrelly in scrapbook in Sheehy Skeffington papers, NLI, MS 21616-21656. Neither name of paper nor exact date is given, but 1911 is written in pencil in margin.
5   *Bean na hÉireann* April 1909.
6   Hanna Sheehy Skeffington, Reminiscences, p.26.
7   *Sligo Champion* 26 December 1896.
8   *Bean na hÉireann* July 1909, written under her pen-name of Maca.
9   Elizabeth Cady Stanton, 'Selections from the History of Woman Suffrage', *The Feminist Papers*, ed. Alice S. Rossi, (2nd edition New York 1974) pp 413–58.
10   *Irish Independent* 2 June 1914.
11   *Freeman's Journal* 30 May 1914.
12   *Irish Independent* 28 May 1914.
13   *Irish Citizen* 28 March 1914 and 9 May 1914.
14   Sheehy Skeffington papers, NLI, MS 34133 (iii).
15   *Irish Citizen* 2 May 1914.
16   Lil Conlon, *Cumann na mBan and the Women of Ireland (1913-25)* (Kilkenny 1969) p.7.
17   Copy of letter from P.H. Pearse to C. Doyle 30 November 1913, NLI, MS 10486.
18   *Irish Volunteer* 4 April 1914.
19   Jacqueline van Voris, *Constance de Markievicz in the Cause of Ireland* (University of Massachusetts Press 1967) p. 132.

20   *Irish Citizen* 11 April 1914. At a meeting of Galway City branch of Cumann na mBan in August 1914, a Dr Walsh regretted that only a hundred men had joined the Volunteer, and asked the ladies to use their influence to get their brothers and sweethearts to join (*Irish Volunteer* 15 August 1914).

21   ibid. 2 May 1914.

22   *Freeman's Journal* 6 May 1914.

23   *Irish Volunteer* 9 May 1914.

24   *Irish Independent* 8 May 1914.

25   ibid.

26   *Irish Citizen* 4 July 1914.

27   ibid. May 1919.

28   ibid. 8 August 1914.

Solidarity

1   *Irish Citizen* February 1918.

2   F.S.L. Lyons, *Ireland Since the Famine* (Fontana, Great Britain, rev. ed. 1973) p.386; *Irish Citizen* June, July and August 1917.

3   Lyons op. cit. p.389.

4   *Irish Citizen* July 1918; *IWFL Report 1917*.

5   Minutes of the Conference of Women Delegates to the all-Ireland conference, 12 May 1917, later known as Cumann na Teactaire (Sheehy Skeffington papers, NLI, MS 21194).

6   ibid. copy of letter sent to Sinn Fein executive, 1 August 1917. The women proposed by the delegates were Kathleen Clarke, Áine Ceannt, Kathleen Lynn, Jennie Wyse Power, Helena Molony, Mrs Ginnell.

7   ibid. 17 September 1917.

8   ibid. 25 September 1917. These minutes refer to the fact that Dr Lynn had written an article urging women to assert their political rights, given them in the Republican Proclamation. This article had been sent to *Nationality*, but not published. The meeting to have the article printed as a handbill or pamphlet.

9   ibid. 2 October 1917.

10   ibid. 16 October 1917. These minutes also note that Kathleen Lynn had been attending Sinn Féin executive meetings as proxy for Countess Plunkett during the latter's illness. On her recovery the committee considered it desirable to maintain Dr Lynn as a delegate, and Áine Ceannt withdrew in her favour. The four women delegates from the group from this date were therefore, Jennie Wyse Power, Kathleen Lynn, Grace Plunkett, and Helena Molony. Countess Plunkett had been a member of the steering committee from its inception.

11   *Irish Citizen* November 1917.

12   Cumann na Teactaire minutes 2 April 1918, General Meeting.

13   ibid. 26 February 1918 and 26 March 1918.
14   ibid. 2 April 1918.
15   Cumann na Teactaire minutes 14 February 1918.
16   ibid. 30 January 1919.
17   Brian Farrell, *The Founding of Dáil Éireann: Parliament and Nation-Building* (Gill & MacMillan Ltd., Dublin 1971) p.11.
18   Cumann na Teactaire minutes, 26 February 1918.
19   *Irish Citizen* 12 September 1914.
20   Sheehy Skeffington papers, NLI, MS 22672 (1).
21   *Irish Citizen* October 1916.
22   ibid. September 1918.
23   Jacqueline van Voris op. cit. p.243.
24   *Irish Citizen* September 1918.
25   Sheehy Skeffington papers, NLI, MS 24191; also *Irish Citizen* September 1918.
26   *Irish Citizen* July 1918.
27   ibid. April 1919. IWFL *Annual Report* 1918.
28   *Sinn Féin* 21 September 1907.
29   Cumann na Teactaire minutes 26 February 1918.
30   ibid. 26 March 1918.
31   *Irish Citizen* August 1918.
32   ibid. April 1919; *IWFL Report 1918*. As a result of all this activity, yet another society was formed – this one for the protection of Ireland from VD.
33   ibid.

Victory – The Vote

1   *Irish Citizen* May 1919, extract from talk given to IWFL by Margaret Connery on 'The Future of Feminism'.
2   Rosen op. cit. p.266.
3   *Irish Citizen* July 1918.
4   ibid. December 1918.
5   *ITUC Report* for 1918.
6   *Sinn Féin, An Appeal to the Women of Ireland* (Dublin 1918).
7   *Sinn Féin 10th Convention Report*, 25 October 1917.
8   Farrell op. cit. p.27.
9   *Irish Citizen* December 1918.
10   Sheehy Skeffington papers, NLI, MS 24107.
11   *Irish Citizen* April 1919.
12   Cumann na Teactaire minutes, 30 January 1919.
13   *Irish Citizen* February 1920.
14   ibid. September-December 1920 (The paper had just recently become a quarterly).
15   Marie Johnson memoirs, op. cit.

16 *Dáil Éireann, Minutes of Proceedings*, 2 March 1922, pp 197–214.

17 P.S. O'Hegarty, *The Victory of Sinn Féin* (Talbot Press, Dublin, 1924) pp 56-8 and 102-5.

18 Maurice Manning, 'Women in Irish Natioanl and Local Politics 1922-77' *Women in Irish Society*, p.92 (see ch.1 fn 7).

19 *Irish Citizen* October 1919.

20 ibid. November 1917.

21 Mary E. Daly art. cit. p.78.

22 Molony art. cit. p. 31.

23 Manning art. cit. p.99.

Bibliography

MANUSCRIPT SOURCES IN IRISH LIBRARIES

NATIONAL LIBRARY OF IRELAND:
S. Czira Papers. Christina M. Doyle – letters. Bulmer Hobson Papers. J. F. X. O'Biren Papers. William O'Brien Papers. John Redmond Papers. Sheehy Skeffington Papers. Women's Suffrage Exhibition Material.
TRINITY COLLEGE:
John Dillon Papers.
LIBRARY OF THE SOCIETY OF FRIENDS, EUSTACE ST., DUBLIN.
Letters and press cuttings re Thomas and Anna Haslam.

STATE ARCHIVES

STATE PAPER OFFICE OF IRELAND:
General Prison's Board, Suffragette Papers, 1912–14. Chief Secretary's Office, Registered Papers. Chief Secretary's Office, Police and Crime Reports 1886–1915.

OTHER ARCHIVES

NATIONAL MUSEUM OF IRELAND (NMI):
Notebook belonging to Constance de Markievicz.

MANUSCRIPT SOURCES IN LIBRARIES OUTSIDE IRELAND

Asquith Papers (papers of Herbert Henry, First Earl   of Oxford and Asquith) Bodleian Library, Oxford. Balfour Papers (papers of Arthur J. Balfour) British Library. Fawcett Papers (papers of Dame Millicent Garrett Fawcett) Fawcett Library, London. Gladstone Papers (papers of Herbert, Viscount Gladstone) British Library. Henry Devenish Harben correspondence 1912–14 (contains letters by Christabel and Sylvia Pankhurst) British Library. Lloyd George Papers (papers of David Earl Lloyd-George of Dwyfor) Record Office, House of Lords, London. London Society for Women's Suffrage, Correspondence, Fawcett Library, London. David Mitchell collection (London Museum). Shaw Papers (papers of G. B. Shaw), British Library. Women's Suffrage Collection, Manchester Public Library.

PARLIAMENTARY PAPERS

Parl. Deb. 4th and 5th series, House of Commons. Parl. Deb. 4th series, House of Lords.

DAIL EIREANN

Dail Eireann, Minutes of Proceedings 2 March 1922.

ANNUAL REPORTS

Irish Women's Suffrage and Local Government Association, Report of the Executive Committee 1876–1918. Irish Women's Suffrage Federation, Annual Reports 1912–17. Irish Women's Franchise League, Report of Executive Committee for 1913. Irish Central Bureau for the Employment of Women, Annual Reports 1906–17

SUFFRAGE PERIODICALS

IRISH:
The Irish Citizen. The Women's Advocate.

ENGLISH:
Alexandra Magazine and Englishwomen's Journal. The Common Cause. Englishwomen's Journal. The Vote. Votes for Women. Women's Suffrage Journal.

EUROPEAN:
Jus Suffragii.

NON-SUFFRAGE PERIODICALS

Bean na hEireann. The Catholic Bulletin. The Leader. the Leprachaun. Shan Van Vocht. St. Stephens. The National Student.

NEWSPAPERS

Belfast Newsletter. Dublin Evening Mail. Enniscorthy Echo. Evening Herald. Evening Telegraph. Freeman's Journal. Irish Citizen. Irish Freedom. Irish Independent. Irish Labour Journal. Irish Press. Irish Times. Irish Volunteer. Irish Worker. Kildare Observer. Leinster Leader. Sligo Champion. Workers Republic.

OFFICIAL REPORTS

Report of Commission on Vocational Organisation Dublin 1943 .

BOOKS

•Blackburn, Helen *A handy book of reference for Irishwomen,* London 1888. *Women's Suffrage, A Record of the Women's Suffrage Movement in the British Isles,* London 1902

•Bradshow, M *Open Doors for Irishwomen,* Dublin 1907

•Colum, Mary *Life and the Dream,* New York 1947

•Concannon, Helena *Daughters of Banba,* Dublin 1930 (2nd ed)

•Cousins, J. H. & M. E *We Two Together,* Madras, India, 1950

•Cousins, Mary F *Woman's Work in Modern Society,* Kenmare 1874

•Dangerfield, George *The Strange Death of Liberal England,* London 1966

•Davis, Richard, *Arthur Griffith and non-violent Sinn Fein,* Dublin 1974

•Edwards, O Dudley & Pyle, F. (ed)., *1916 The Easter Rising,* London

•Edwards, R. Dudley, *A New History of Ireland,* Dublin 1972

•Edwards, R. Dudley, *An Atlas of Irish History,* London 1973

•Evans, R. J *The Feminists: Women's Emancipation Movements in Europe, America and Australasia, 1840–1920,* London 1977

•Farrell, Brian *The Founding of Dail Eireann: Parliament and Nation-Building,* Dublin 1971

•Fitzgerald, W. J *The Voice of Ireland,* Dublin, Manchester & London, 1924

•Fox, R. M *Louie Bennett: Her Life and Times,* Dublin 1957. *Rebel Irishwomen,* Dublin 1967 (2nd ed). *Jim Larkin,* London 1957

•Fulford, Roger *Votes for Women,* London 1957

•Greaves, C. Desmond *The Irish Transport and General Workers' Union – The Formative Years, 1909–1923,* Dublin 1982

•Horne, Rt. Rev. George, *Reflections on the Importance of Forming the Female Character by Education,* Dublin 1796

•Keogh, Dermot *The Rise of the Irish Working Class,* Belfast 1982

•Kohn, L *The Constitution of the Irish Free State,* London 1932

•Larkin, E *James Larkin, Irish Labour Leader 1876–1947,* 1961

•Lloyd, Trevor *Suffragettes International,* London 1971

•Lyons, F. S. L *Ireland Since the Famine,* Dublin 1971. *The Irish Parliamentary Party 1890–1910,* 1951

•Laurence, Margaret *We Write as Women,* London 1937

•Martin, F. X. and Byrne, F. J. (ed) *The Scholar Revolutionary: Eoin MacNeill, 1867–1945,* Shannon, 1973

•Mitchell, David *The Fighting Pankhursts,* London 1967

•MacBride, M. Gonne *A Servant of the Queen,* (1st ed) London 1938

•McCarthy, Charles *Trade Unions in Ireland 1894–1960,* Dublin 1977

•O'Brien, C. Cruise, *States of Ireland 1974* (2nd ed)

•O'Neill, William L *The Woman Movement: Feminism in the United States and England,* London and New York 1969

•O'Hegarty, P. S *The Victory of Sinn Fein,* Dublin 1924

•Pankhurst, Christabel *Unshackled,* London 1959

•Pankhurst, Emmeline *My Own Story,* London 1914

•Rosen, Andrew *Rise Up Women!* London and Boston 1974

•Rossi, A. S. (ed) *The Feminist Papers,* New York 1973

•Rover, Constance *Women's Suffrage and Party Politics in Britain 1866–1914,* London 1967

•Rowbotham, Sheila *Women Resistance and Revolution,* (2nd ed) 1974

•Ryan, W. P *The Pope's Green Island,* London 1912

•Somerville, E. and Martin, V *Irish Memories,* London 1917

•Snowden, E *The Feminist Movement,* (n.d.) London and Glasgow

•Tierney, M *Struggle with Fortune,* Dublin 1954

•Tynan, Katherine *The Years of the Shadow,* London 1919

•Thompson, William. *Appeal of one Half the Human Race, Women, Against the Pretensions of the Other Half Men, To Retrain Them in Political, and Thence in*

Civil and Domestic Slavery, In reply to a paragraph of Mr. Mill's celebrated articles on Government, Cork 1975 (2nd ed)

•Van Voris, J   *Constance de Markievicz in the Cause of Ireland,* Massachusetts 1967

•Ward, Margaret   *Unmanageable Revolutionaries, Women and Irish Nationalism,* Kerry, 1983

ARTICLES

•Barry, Rev. D   'Female Suffrage from a Catholic Standpoint', *Irish Ecclesiastical Record,* Vol XXVI, September 1909

•Boyd, E. A   'Feminism and Woman Suffrage', *The Irish Review,* November 1913

•Breathnach, Eibhlin, *'Women and Higher Education in Ireland 1879–1914', The Crane Bag,* Vol. 4, No. 1, 1980

•Brooke, W. G   'Report on the differences in the law of England and Ireland as regards the protection of Women', *Journal of the Statistical and Social Inquiry Society of Ireland* Vol 111, April 1973 'Endowments for Higher Education of Girls', *Journal of the Statistical and Social Inquiry Society of Ireland* Vol VI, April 1873

•"W.F.B." 'Trinity College and Lady Students: a plea for the higher education of Women', *Dublin University Review,* March 1885

•Clery, Prof. A. E   'The Religious aspect of Women's Suffrage', *The Irish Review,* November 1913. 'Votes for Youth', *Studies,* June 1915

•d'Alton, Ian   'Southern Irish Unionism', *Transactions of the Royal Historical Society,* 5th series, 23, 1973

•Daly, Mary E   'Women in the Irish Workforce from Pre-Industrial to Modern Times', *Saothar 7,*   1981

•"F.J.F." 'The Education of Girls', *Dublin University Magazine,* January 1871

•Gibson, E   'Employment of Women in Ireland', *Journal of the Statistical and Social Inquiry Society of Ireland,* Vol 111, April 1862

•Houston, Prof   'The extension of the field for the employment of women', *Journal of the Statistical and Social Inquiry Society of Ireland,* Vol IV, November 1866

•Lee, J. J   'Women and the Church since the Famine', *Women in Irish Society, The Historical Dimension,* 1978

Lavery, R   'The future of Irishwomen', *New Ireland Review,* December 1909

•McCraith, L. M   'Irishwomen and their Vote', *The New Ireland Review,* Vol XXX, December 1908

•MacCurtain, Margaret   'Towards an Appraisal of the Religious Image of Women', *The Crane Bag,* Vol 4, No. 1, 1980

•Manning, Maurice   'Women in Irish National and Local Politics 1922–77', *Women in Irish Society, The Historical Dimension,* 1978

•Mill, James   'Government', *Encyclopaedia Britanica,* Supplement to 4th, 5th and 6th editions, Vol No. 4, 1820

•Murray, Peter 'Electoral Politics and the Dublin Working Class before the First World War', *Saothar 6*, 1980

•Molony, Helena 'James Connolly and Women', *Dublin Labour Year Book 1930*

•Oldham, A 'Women and the Irish University question', *The New Ireland Review*, Vol VI, January 1897

•Owens, Rosemary 'Votes for Ladies, Votes for Women; Organised Labour and the Suffrage Movement, 1876–1922', *Saothar 9*, Journal of the Irish Labour History Society, 1983

•Ryan, F 'The Suffrage Tangle', *The Irish Review*, September 1912

•Sheehy Skeffington, H 'The Woman's Movement in Ireland', *Irish Review*, July 1912. 'Review of 'Our Freedom and its Results'', *Ireland Today*, November 1936. 'Women in Politics', *The Bell*, November 1943

•Snoddy, O 'Suffragettes in Carlow', *Carloviana*, December 1964

•Webb, A., 'The Propriety of conceding the Elective Franchise to Woman', *Journal of the Statistical and Social Inquiry Society of Ireland*, Vol IV, January 1868

Unsigned: 'How the women of a country can influence its destiny', *Dublin University Magazine*, May 1839. 'The Women of Ireland', *Dublin University Magazine*, May 1839. 'Womanhood and its Mission', *Dublin University Magazine*, May 1859. 'Women and Work', *Dublin University Magazine*, December 1872. 'The Education of Women', *Dublin University Magazine*, May 1874

PAMPHLETS (IN IRISH LIBRARIES)

•Butt, Isaac *The Poor Law Bill for Ireland examined*, 1837

•Connolly, J *labour in Ireland* Dublin 1934

•Day, S. R *Women in the New Ireland* n.d., published for Munster Women's Franchise League, Cork, c 1912

•Despard, C *Theosophy and the Women's Movement*, London 1913

•Fox, R *Marx, Engels, Lenin on the Irish Revolution*, London 1932

•Gossan, N. J *A Plea for the Ladies*, Dublin 1875

•Haslam, T. J *Women's Suffrage from a Masculine Standpoint*, Dublin 1906 . *Some last words on Women's Suffrage*, Dublin 1916

•de Markievicz, C *Women, Ideals and the Nation*, Dublin 1909

•Pius XII, *Women's Place in The World* 1945

•Sheehy Skeffington, A. D. and Owens, R *Votes for Women*, Dublin 1975

•Sinn Fein *An Appeal to the Women of Ireland*, Dublin 1918 . *10th Convention Report*, 25 October 1917

•Stanley, Wm., *The Unexpurgated case against Woman Suffrage*, London, November 1913

the Balance, Publication of Bedford College, London, November 1913

PAMPHLETS AND LEAFLETS IN LIBRARIES OUTSIDE IRELAND

BRITISH LIBRARY:

British and Irish Ladies Society for improving the condition and promoting the industry and welfare of the female peasantry in Ireland, *Annual Reports* 1823–28
Address given to College Historical Society, University of Dublin, 14 November 1894, by A. E. Simms
Irish Women's Suffrage and Local Govt. Association, leaflets. (i) Paper read at Conference of Poor Law Guardians, Dublin, 19 April 1900. (ii) Paper read at Conference of Poor Law Guardians, Dublin 1903. (iii) Report of executive committee for 1910. (iv) Suggestions for intending women workers under the Local Government Act, 1901.
Queen's Institute, 13th and 14th *Annual Reports* of Queen's Institute and Queen's College for education of Women, 1876

FAWCETT LIBRARY:
•Bourke, John W The Emancipation of Women (essay read at the Cork Literary and Scientific Society in 1870–71 session)
•Chapman, Rev. and Hugh B The Soul of Woman Suffrage (address given under the auspices of the I.W.R.L., 16 April 1912 in Dublin)
•"Ephedros", The economic aspect of Woman Suffrage (published for I.W.R.L., n.d.)
•Garvey, E The Position of Irishwomen in Local Administration (1896)
•Gwynne, Mrs. S How Women can use the Vote (published by I.C.W.S.A.)
•Mahon, Catherine Women Teachers and the Vote (address given to I.C.W.S.A.)
•Redmond, W. and Kettle, T Pamphlet issued by N.U.W.S.S. – Speeches on Parliamentary Franchise (Woman) Bill 1910
•Robertson, Miss A. I Women's need of Representation (Dublin 1872)
•Ross, Rev. J. Elliott An American Priest on Votes for Women, pub. by I.C.W.S.A. 1915
•Shaw, Bernard, Sir Almroth Wright's case against Women's Suffrage answered (reprinted from the *New Statesman* for I.W.S.F.)

THESIS:

•Breathnach, Eibhlinn A History of the Movement for Women's Higher Education in Dublin 1860–1912, (Unpublished M.A. thesis, University College Dublin, 1981)

Attic Press is a dynamic and innovative feminist publishing house which aims to publish books by women and about women. For too long Ireland has ignored the full potential of women's writings, which have been lost to anonymity and foreign publishing. Our aim is to reclaim this material and fill the gap.

If you would like to know more about Attic or our books write to us at 48 Fleet Street, Dublin 2.

NEW AND FORTHCOMING TITLES

THE BEST OF NELL: A selection of writings over fourteen years by Nell McCafferty. Introduced by Eavan Boland.
The Best of Nell is a funny and sad book which will place Nell McCafferty along side the top international journalists whose work deserves to be recorded in a more permanent book form.
£3.95pb £9.50hb

SMASHING TIMES: A History of the Irish Women's Suffrage Movement 1898 — 1922.
Rosemary Cullen Owens
Who were the women involved in the early women's movement? How did they set about obtaining their objectives? How were they viewed? What was achieved? *Smashing Times* traces the development of the early feminist movement in Ireland and attempts to answer some of these questions.
£4.95pb £10.00hb

HAIRY STRIPS CARTOONS
Arja Kajermo
Arja's cartoons are funny, amusing, satirical and downright hilarious. This second book of her unique style of cartoon is an ideal way to give yourself or someone else a good laugh.
£2.95pb

WOMEN STUDYING WOMEN: Collected Essays in Womens' Studies.
Edited by Liz Steiner-Scott
£5.95pb £15.00hb

AROUND THE BANKS OF PIMLICO
Mairin Johnson
£4.95pb £12.50hb

Back List
MISSING PIECES: Women in Irish History
£2.00pb
SINGLED OUT: Single Mothers in Ireland
£1.95pb